IT'S FINE
IT'S ~~FINE~~
IT'S ~~FINE~~

TAZ ALAM

IT'S FINE
IT'S ~~FINE~~
IT'S ~~FINE~~

(it's not)

HarperCollins*Publishers*

HarperCollins*Publishers*
1 London Bridge Street
London SE1 9GF

www.harpercollins.co.uk

HarperCollins*Publishers*
1st Floor, Watermarque Building, Ringsend Road
Dublin 4, Ireland

First published by HarperCollins*Publishers* 2021

10 9 8 7 6 5 4 3 2 1

Text © Taz Alam 2021
Illustrations © Shamima Ahmed 2021

Taz Alam asserts the moral right to be identified as the author of this work

A catalogue record of this book is available from the British Library

ISBN 978-0-00-850138-9

Printed and bound in the UK using 100% renewable electricity at CPI Group (UK) Ltd

MIX
Paper from
responsible sources
FSC™ C007454
FSC
www.fsc.org

This book is produced from independently certified FSC™ paper to ensure responsible forest management.

For more information visit: www.harpercollins.co.uk/green

I wrote this book for my younger self, and for anyone who feels
or has felt scared, isolated and alone like younger Taz did.
I hope you feel understood and comforted by these pages in
the same way I did when writing them.

Contents

it's not fine

MY NOTE TO YOU

Growing up, I struggled with a lot of difficult emotions. I never felt like I had anyone to talk to about the things I was going through, which led me to feel isolated and alone.

That is why I wanted to write this poetry book.

I wanted to talk about things I wish I was able to hear when I was younger that might have helped me growing up. This book is honest and real; it will make you feel seen and understood. More importantly, it will assure you that what you're feeling is normal, valid and okay.

Life can be joyous and empowering but also difficult and confusing at times. Let's talk openly about how we feel and navigate life's challenges together.

Taz x

HOW TO USE THIS BOOK

This book is a safe space for you to feel whatever you're feeling without judgement.

There will be moments of joy, love and purpose, but there'll also be moments where the journey is tough and it feels a little too real. Life can get a little too much at times, I understand, but know that you don't have to go through it alone.

Let this book be your comfort to help you process the emotions that come with life.

If you're feeling in need of uplift, a hug or a friend, the chapters *Healing* (page 175) and *I'm Fine* (page 219) are a great place to start!

There are poems that touch on sensitive topics that may be triggering. We're mindful of your needs, so if you're feeling particularly vulnerable and fragile, you'll find those poems marked with a plaster (see above) to highlight their sensitive nature. The chapter *It's Not Fine* (page 71) deals with some tough topics that can be difficult to process. That's okay; it's important to always take care of yourself.

Whether you're feeling lost, confused, scared, struggling with relationships – this book will help you feel seen, validated and understood. Feel free to come here whenever you want comfort and a safe space to process your emotions.

Life can be difficult to navigate so let's work through it, together.

WHO AM I ?

(self love / questioning myself / body image)

who am i?

Sometimes I question
what I'm doing with my life.

Am I happy?
Am I content?
                Or am I living a life
                I didn't ask for
                And will one day
                look back on and resent?

It's funny isn't it,
Life demands so much
from you,
but rarely
ever asks your consent.

From birth you're trained,
To think a certain way.
From how you dress,
your education,
to the things you say.
                It's all conditioned.
                It's been ingrained.

But then you grow up
and start to think for yourself,

3

And suddenly you look around,
and no one's there to help.

You start to question things about your life,
Slowly things start to change.
You have these innate desires and
thoughts you can't always explain.

You no longer align with
the plan set out for you
and for some reason
that makes you feel strange.
You're filled with so much guilt
just for thinking a different way.

But you can't deny,
        deep down inside,
            something just doesn't feel right.

And sadly we grow up,
life takes over
and we give up the fight.

We do as we're told,
give in to society and
eventually, the light inside us dies.
It almost seems inevitable at this point,
we've seen it happen too many times.

I've struggled with this feeling a lot,
Constantly battling with myself.
Doing everything society wanted from me
Till it affected my mental health.

We give so much of ourselves away,
only for people to judge.

We sacrifice our souls and wonder why
we never feel good enough.

Imagine instead of trying so hard to fit in,
we focused on self-love.
Maybe then we wouldn't
be so quick to give up.

I can't fight   this feeling anymore.
I can't repress   the person in me,

                                    screaming to be let out.

Everyone settles
and accepts this way of life

                            but the silence is too loud.

I want to escape,
I want to run,
I want to drown the noise and shout.
I want to live.
I want to know what life's truly about.

I want to rediscover myself,
Create the person I'm meant to be.
Decondition everything I've been taught,
To finally feel free.

We only get one chance at life,
we owe it to ourselves to at least try,
Yeah we could sink and fail,
but maybe ...
                  just maybe ...
                                    We can fly.

am i scared?

am I scared?
                absolutely terrified.

but not as scared as living
                        and never feeling alive.

charades

I've spent my whole life playing roles,
Changing myself to suit other people's needs.
I learned that is how you survive in this world.
If you want to get somewhere in life
then you need to people please.

At times life feels like a game of charades,
I wake up and think what character will I play today?
I question if I'm even living for myself,
Is this really what I would think, and say?

It's strange.
I can so easily adapt and change.
But one person I've never known is myself.
Who even am I at this stage?

why do we choose to hate ourselves?

Why do we refuse to give ourselves love,
But are so adamant on bringing ourselves down?
Why is it that between love and hate,
The latter always takes the crown?

Why are we so comfortable seeing our own downfall?
Why are we so afraid to be kind to ourselves?
We're so consumed by these unrealistic standards,
That we'd rather prioritise other people's opinions
than our own mental health.

But what if we dared to be rebellious?
What if we stood up and were brave?
We finally decided to love ourselves,
I wonder how much our lives would change?

I want to shower myself with abundant love.
I want to relish denial for a while.
I want to see life from a different perspective,
Take on life with a smile.
Hating myself is exhausting.
I want to know what it feels like to matter.
Between hate and happiness,
I want to choose the latter.

it's complicated

Humans are complicated.
Yet we package ourselves in a perfect way
To make it easier for people to digest
to make them feel comfortable.
We put on our daily mask,
remove ourselves of flaws
and anything remotely vulnerable.

Why is society fascinated with perfection
when humans are inherently complicated?

Why do we feel the need to hide our imperfections,
almost as if we're obligated?

We're an amalgamation of our experiences, environment,
    behaviours instilled in us from a young age.
All of this happens
    before we even start to think for ourselves.
We spend our adult lives living
    with a version of ourselves we had
little choice in creating,
    and navigating life
with little to no help.

As we become self-aware
we start to hate ourselves for
the way we think,
    the things we do,
        the way we behave.
The emotions become overwhelming
and we're filled with guilt and shame.
The anger inside builds
and the frustration gets harder to tame.

For anyone who can relate,
I need you to know that
you're not to blame.

Some of us spend our whole adult lives
unlearning what we were taught.
But it's tough.
We try to repress our ugly,
repress our broken,
But some days the work
doesn't feel enough.

You become guarded with your space
when really you're just protecting,
Or become so overwhelmed with the emotions
That you resort to projecting.
It sucks because you never asked to be this way.
You never asked for any of it,
yet you've been left to fix the pain.

Some bad memories linger like cheap perfume.
     And no matter how much you try to restrain –
every now and again they escape.

They come out screaming and reveal themselves
in the most raw and darkest ways,
To serve as a harsh reminder
that you can never truly get away.
This is something you have to live with
and the pain is here to stay.

why?

Why do we tear ourselves apart trying to please people who have never once tried to listen or take the time to understand us?

compare myself

I know I shouldn't compare,
But when I scroll through social media
I can't help but stop and stare.
Looking at all the perfect lives on my screen,
feeling like life is unfair,
And I keep feeding this unhealthy habit
until I can no longer bear.

I know it's no good for me
yet I continue to seek it out –
then beat myself up.
It's a losing game that I'm addicted to,
An unhealthy obsession,
and I can't get enough.

Everyone seems so ahead in life.
People who are younger than me
are more successful.
It's like I'm so behind in life that I'm
constantly playing catch-up,
And living has become
so incredibly stressful.

I want to hide from the world.
I feel like a constant failure.
And I know this isn't a healthy way to cope,
But I don't know how to correct this behaviour.

i hate myself

I hate myself.
I hate my face.
I hate my body.
I hate the environment that I'm in.
I'm filled with so much
hate I don't know what
To do with all of it.

I look at models in magazines and when
I look back at myself,
I no longer like what I see.
They don't show you the stretch marks,
split ends, gap teeth,
They don't represent people
Like you and me.

Isn't it ironic how we're forced messages like
'be yourself' by manufactured celebrities,
when they know they're partially
to blame for all our insecurities?
If we do *this*, say *that*,
and wear *this* then
a guy might just like me.
I can't hold a conversation
without saying the word sorry,
like, 15 gazillion times, to say that,
I'm apologising for just being me.

Some days the silence is so loud
it keeps me up at night.
I can't sleep or eat.
Filled with so much negativity
until negativity became me.

But I lie and carry on smiling
because that's the person I want to be –
so happy, joyful and carefree.

People say, *just be confident*,
they don't understand that
   you get tired,
     you get weak.
I just need you to see that
I'm filled with self-hate
and it consumes me.

Because I wasn't brought up to be
proud of myself and love who I am.
No, I was told there were
expectations and limitations
and fought for every *can't* to be a *can*.

So filled with hate I suffocate,
This is my fate ... I tell myself as
I try to pick myself up but it's
too late.

I don't want compliments or attention from passers by,
I crave real love,
not likes.

You know, you start to create this self-image that is
so perfect
so flawless
so happy
Because you think
that's what is right.

Wrong.

See, you can't fill a void with lies,
you can't resolve pain with short highs,
So you resort to late-night cries
and you wonder why?

Sigh.

For the longest time I would blame
my environment, the media, my peers.
And it took me years
to see that it's not you,

it's me.

If I want to change how I feel
I have to start from within.
Look into my soul,
what's beneath the skin.

You can't solve your problems
From scrolling on your phone.
The answer comes from
Who you are deep inside.
All those thoughts and feelings
You tried so desperately to hide.
I am capable of so much more
and I don't need to hear that from you
because I know it, for me.

See, when you open your mind
You start to see things clearly,
Your potential, ambitions and dreams
You become free.
So, for the first time in a long time
I'm just going to let myself breathe.

Today, I choose me.

i'm ugly

You keep telling yourself that you're ugly,
How you can't possibly love yourself
because every time you look in the mirror,
you don't like what you see.

The stretch marks, loose skin, gap between your front teeth,
overanalysing every single part of yourself,
battering your self-esteem,
constantly telling yourself
how could anyone ever want you,
When even you don't like your own body?

I wish I could make you understand that you're perfect,
just by being you,
and I'd tell you that every single day,
until you start to believe it too.

And I mean it,
I just wish you knew
how much I adore you.
How I love that even when you're going through
some of your toughest times,
you still put all of your energy into
putting on a smile
and acting like everything's fine.

Or how I think you're brave, intelligent, gentle, kind,
how you're going to change the world someday
with that incredible mind.

I hate seeing you cry
because when you look in the mirror
you see something you don't like,
and I hate how much it hurts you every single time.
I wish I could take your pain away,
make you see what I see,
and then maybe you'd change your mind.

I hate watching you beat yourself up all the time.
When are you going to realise that
this ongoing battle you have with yourself,
   it's a losing fight?
You're literally destroying yourself from the inside.
  Trying so hard to be something you're not,
when you're already perfectly fine.
You're a beautiful, walking,
human sunshine in my eyes.

You keep comparing yourself to others,
when are you going to understand
that being yourself is enough?
You keep seeking validation from other people,
when what you really need is self-love.

Yes I know you don't have the perfect body,
    reality check, most people don't.
So, what's the use in tearing yourself apart like this?
If you think it's going to help you in anyway,
well let me be the first to tell you – it won't.

I'll never understand how someone so great
    can think so little about themselves.
I watch you, unable to leave the house without make-up,
    struggling to cope everyday,
and I just want to be able to help.

You've reduced yourself to ugly.
You hide behind baggy clothes, watch what you eat,
Care so much about what people think
that you can't even walk down the street,
self-hate has filtered its way through
to every inch of your body,
and it kills me
to see someone I care about
be so incredibly unhappy.

I hope one day you can look in the mirror
and live with what you see,
that it doesn't hurt you so much anymore,
because you understand that you've got more to offer
to the world than simply being pretty.
No longer haunted by the scars on your skin,
but fighting to be the change they want to see.

But more importantly,
Right now, in this moment,
I want you to know
just how incredibly perfect you are to me.

fat

Society will tell you
if you're fat then you're worthless and lazy.
You do not deserve a man who's way out of your league.
Because they're reserved for the 'beautiful people',
you know, the ones who are tall and skinny
with defined collar bones and a thigh gap
for the whole world to see.

See, we are conditioned to think that
those are the only things that make a person 'pretty',
worthy of being seen on television,
social media and fashion magazines.

See, fat people don't belong in that world.
They've been told to wear big jumpers and baggy tees,
The type of clothes that cover every inch of their body.
See, they're not designed for crop tops or short sleeves.
It's become clear that popular clothing stores
do not cater for curvaceous physiques.

Just the word fat sounds so negative and ugly.
It's as if the media refuses to accept that
these people are even part of society.
I mean, it's one thing to say they
don't fit in with the modelling industry
But to ignore them completely – is obscene.

See, the reason why this attitude is dangerous,
is because of the impact it has on people mentally.
It creates insecurity and destroys young people's
    self-esteem.
When the world focuses so much on body size
You start to look at yourself differently.
You're more conscious walking down the street,
Filled with guilt, you start watching what you eat,
obsessively counting calories.

It's everywhere you go,
the shopping centre, at school, the library,
People shaming you, blaming you,
such hate when they speak.

And you hear it so often, that even you start to believe it
Thinking to yourself, *maybe the problem is me.*
Society has made you feel like
a prisoner in your own body.

From a young age girls and boys grow up
hating the body that they're in.
Feeling guilty when they binge,
like they've committed a sin.
Thinking that the only way they'll ever be happy
is if only, just for one day,
they knew what it felt like to be thin.
Believing that that will take all their problems away,
when in reality, it doesn't work that way.

True happiness comes from within
and to do that you need to love the skin you're in,
Any other way and you just won't win.
Just an endless cycle
where you keep sinking

                 and sinking.

We're obsessed with body size.
Search *How to Lose Weight Quickly*
and flick through pages and pages of videos online.
Which is so unhealthy because
These things take time.
If we're skinny then our life will magically
fall into place,
and everything will be
happy and okay.
Wake up, life doesn't work that way.

You are
your character,
your thoughts,
your experiences,
your strength,
your resilience,
your empathy,

                 not your weight.

A generation where people starve themselves thin,
So consumed by expectations and self-hate.
Made to feel like you're not good enough
because you don't look a certain way.

Do we need to tick boxes
to feel self-worth, and only then be respected?
Becoming carbon-copy models, looking perfect on the outside,
but on the inside we are empty.

It's all just a sick game society has made,
and you can either play and live a life
filled with shame and self-hate,
or you can be brave, realise your own truth
And walk away.

Live life your own way.
Have the ultimate say.

If you want to lose weight, great,
Just make sure you do it the healthy way,
and for the right reasons.
Understand that it's a process, and work at it day by day.

I say all of this because,
even though I don't know you, I still care.

When will we realise body positivity is
not about encouraging obesity?
It's about allowing people for once in their life
To accept their body without feeling ashamed or guilty.
So this is why I stress, work on being healthy,
make yourself the priority,
learn to appreciate and love yourself,
and give yourself
a chance to be happy.

i don't want to be me anymore

I have this idea of myself.
A version of me that I adore.
She's starting to feel like a
Figment of my imagination
And now I worry I'm stuck with
The version that is flawed.

I've lived with this person
For a while now.
She's alright, but
I'm starting to get bored.

All she does is cry and
Feel sorry for herself.
I don't know if I want
To be her anymore.

labels

Can we denormalise reducing ourselves to labels?
It's okay to experiment and suddenly switch tables.
I am whoever I feel and choose to be on that day.
Tomorrow I may feel differently, and that is also okay.

version of me

I see the version of me on people's screen,
And she is so happy and bright.
She makes people feel better
and helps them get through their day,
Not a single flaw in sight.

But I wonder,
If they saw the version of me
behind closed doors,
would they feel the same?
Would they accept me,
broken pieces and all,
Or would they run away?

body

I want to apologise to my body.
I'm sorry for all the hate I subjected you to.
I'm sorry for not giving you
the love and appreciation you deserved,
When you were the only thing
that carried me through.

I'm sorry for reducing you to a size,
for giving in to all the pressure
and feeding in to all the lies.
I was hypnotised.
Made to believe I needed to
look a certain way to be satisfied.
I no longer want to feel ashamed or hide.
I'm proud of all you've done for me,
I'm ready to own my body with pride.

MISUNDERSTOOD

(relationships / connection / others)

broken relationship

This room feels so heavy,
So much of what we want to say goes
unspoken.

The tension is so palpable, it's suffocating.
We're too afraid to admit this relationship is
broken.

vulnerability

It seems like everyone is seeking connection,
    But no one is willing to be vulnerable.
Everyone wants to feel close,
    But no one is willing to do the work to get to
a place where they feel comfortable.

If you want to truly feel something
then you need to understand,
That in life it's give and take.
I know you've been hurt before,
    But you're not going to get anywhere
By putting up walls and acting fake.

What are you so scared about?
That people will see you as weak, that people will judge?
    But are other people's judgements worth sacrificing
A life filled with genuine love?

toxic love

I gave you everything and it still wasn't enough.
  It was never ever enough.
You made me feel like I was nothing.
Made me believe
that I was difficult to love.

And like a fool I kept trying,
I kept trying till it became too much.
I got in so deep that I lost who I was.
  I knew it was toxic,
I knew it wasn't right.
But no matter how bad things got,
I couldn't help but try.
I told myself it would be different this time.

I just couldn't give up.
Constantly battling over
whether this is love or lust?
Because if it's love,
Then why was it so messed up?
I would treat myself like nothing,
Yet to you I gave so much.

And then you go and break my heart,
Tell me that you're sorry
and that this is a fresh start.

Like a fool I'd wait
For the day you'd make another mistake.
A part of me wants to speak up,
But I hesitate.
It's like you're controlling me,
you've infected my brain.
How do I escape when
you've become part of my DNA?
Even when you're gone,
I'm still the one left with all the pain.

He said, *he's sorry*.
He told me *he didn't mean it*
and that *he's going to change*.
And I choose to believe him when
he says *he won't hurt me again*.
I'm not expecting you to understand.
Go ahead, judge me.
But if I lose him, I'll have nobody. Do you get that?
Who wants to live a life
where they're alone and empty?
I need him just as much as he needs me.
In some sick twist of fate. He completes me.

That's why it works.
We just keep going until
one of us inevitably gets hurt.

So yeah, I choose to stay. Go ahead and call me weak.
I'm not expecting you to understand,
just know that leaving someone,
It's not that easy.

He's gotten into my mind
and without him I'm paralysed.
To the point where I force myself to believe him
every time he apologises.
Even though I know
It's all lies.

Every waking moment I cry. I've gotten used to it.
It doesn't hurt so much anymore. I've become numb to it.
I've become sore.
And in some sick, twisted way,
He's my only cure.

What can I say?
I'm incredibly flawed.
Love isn't like what you see on TV.
This is what it's like, this is my reality.
It's not as magical as they portray in a Disney movie.
It's a lot of pain and sacrifice.
You just keep pushing until you bleed.

gaslighting

I'm tired.
You make me feel like I've gone insane.
That I'm the problem,
When you're the reason I'm feeling this way.
You make me question my judgment,
Make me think I'm overreacting.
You never admit you're in the wrong,
But rather use tactics that are distracting
Me from the root of the problem.
Always dance around the issues
but never get around to actually solving them.

You make me believe I've gone crazy,
That it's all in my mind.
You manipulate everything,
I can't believe I was so blind
To it all.
You would beat me down
Until I felt so small.

I can't keep up with the constant lies,
I'm tired of having to constantly defend myself.
Being with you is so exhausting,
It's not me, but you, who needs help.

Your words hold no weight,
You apologise only to continue
to make the same mistakes.
You have no intention to change,
We just continue going around this toxic cycle,
it's always the same.
Yet I can never find it in myself to walk away.
Despite how much it hurts me,
I always choose to stay.

allowing you to hurt me

I hate you.
                   But I hate me more
for allowing you
                   to hurt me.

I've learned my lesson.
I'll never again let myself
be this carefree.

i wrote you a letter

I wrote you a letter.
You never replied.
Told me you had a lot going on
and didn't have the time.
I tried to force myself
to believe your lie.

It's been years now and looking at you
no longer hurts.
I've forgotten the sound of your voice,
the way you laughed,
the way you called my name.

Time is the biggest healer, I guess,
And I'm moving on.

But it's scary
how much
has changed.

dear bully

Dear bully,
You control every aspect of my life and have infected my brain,
make me feel so small I start to believe that I'm the one to blame,
like it's my fault things have turned out this way,
and I can't do it anymore, I'm going insane.
I'm serious. I'm done.
I'm tired of always being the victim of your fun.
   I can't take it anymore,
I hope you're happy now, you've won.

When will it stop?
You keep pushing me and pushing me.
Feel like I'm caught up in this wave, struggling to breathe.
Trying so hard to keep my head up, but man,
I'm drowning in this sea.

I just don't know what I did to deserve all of this?
Why do you feel the need to belittle and shame me
   in front of everybody? Is it to make me feel bad?
Because if it is then you're too late, because I hate myself already.

Thanks to you I no longer feel safe,
As I walk down the corridors I can literally feel my heart race,
   You made it very clear that I don't belong in this place.
Constantly going into school terrified,
not knowing what's gonna come my way,

I live each and every day afraid,
and that's all on you.
How can you live with yourself
knowing you treat people this way?
And how messed up must you be
to still think of yourself as great?
You're literally fuelled by negativity and hate.

I may be weak, I may be uncool,
But you find enjoyment from watching people suffer,
What does that say about you?
And everyone laughing along in the crowd, watching someone
*   get bullied,*
you're all just as bad too.
I don't want to live in a world where kids can be so cruel.
So how about you spend less time judging
and more time trying to understand people?
Try and spend a day in their shoes.

I want you to know that your words don't hurt, they bleed,
*   they're not just the bruises on my skin, they cut deep,*
*   infiltrate my mind and haunt me in my sleep.*
They are the sole reason of my constant anxiety.

Thanks to you I started walking with my head down,
*   always nervous, flinching when anyone's around,*
Too scared to raise my voice or make a sound.
Because I know that would lead to trouble.

I can't remember the last time I laughed, or was even happy.
You get so used to being treated like nothing
that it doesn't hurt anymore, you just feel empty.

I have one question – why?
What messed you up so bad that you found enjoyment out of
*   making others cry?*
Thanks to sick people like you, innocent people have died.
Because they feel like there's no way out for them
other than suicide. You know that right?
Do you get some sick pleasure out of that?
Does it make you feel good inside,
knowing your actions are literally destroying lives?
*   How do you live with yourself?*
How do you sleep at night?

This one's for the people who are pushed and shoved,
constantly brought down,
*   made to feel like they're not good enough,*
who, despite their troubles, force themselves to go to school,
*   that's the true definition of tough.*

For those of you going through a rough time right now
I'm sending you a hug, and I know it may not mean much.
But I just want you to know no matter how dark things get,
you are loved. Please, if you're reading this,
Don't
Give
Up.

fake friends

I'm tired of fake friends
Lying behind my back.
Wondering when it'll end,
It seems like fakeness
is the new trend.
Like we're going through the motions,
Just playing pretend.
I keep putting myself out there,
only to be let down again.

Lately it's like I'm always in a room
Filled with people I don't know,
Surrounded by blank faces and feeling so alone.
Putting on a front is exhausting,
Some days I wish I'd just stayed at home.

Just 'friends' on social media,
Trying to get the perfect picture for likes,
Yet in person,
You never seem to treat me right.
Guess it's my fault for choosing
To ignore all the signs,
Live in denial,
Act like everything's fine.

You say you love me online
But never to my face.
I didn't think friendship
Would be this way.

Only here when you need something,
Only here for yourself.
Funny when it's me who's calling,
You're never here to help.

Cancel last minute,
late responses,
no regards to how I feel.
All I've ever wanted is
to feel something real.

Someone who truly cares,
who I can chat for hours with about nonsense,
Someone who will actually be there for me,
My day one,
My constant.

I'm tired of trying to make things work.
I've become so guarded.
Looking at how bad things have become,
Wondering how it started.
I trusted you,
I told you my secrets and that isn't easy.

But then you spoke behind my back
and hung them out like dirty laundry.

For what?
A few moments of laughter.
Yes, you got people talking about me,
    Did it make you feel good after?
Thanks to you I've learned
To keep my mouth shut.
I don't talk about myself
Anymore,
And I regret ever opening up.

I feel so dumb, I didn't have a clue.
It was only when I turned my back,
that I saw the real you.

Opening up only to be let down
Starting to feel like real people don't exist now.
Constantly the butt of the joke
Everyone's laughing and I guess
I'm the clown.
Starting to wonder if
There are any loyal people around.

I should've seen it coming, but
I just wanted to be a part of something.
Sad thing is I've gotten so used to it all
I started to play along.

I put up with it all when I knew
That it was wrong.
Surrounded by so many people
But never once felt like I belonged.
Hoping it would get better, but
I've put up with it for too long.

You don't like me.
That's fine.
I just wish I'd found out sooner
and didn't waste my time.

But you know what,
I deserve better than this.
For once, I'm going to be strong.

I know what I'm worth and
it's more than this.
I think it's time
for me
to move
on.

monster

Fuck it. You win.
This is where the
self-destruction begins.

Go on, hate me,
Tell me all the things that destroy me from the inside.
Remind me of the bad things that will continue
to infiltrate my mind for the rest of time.

You've beaten me down to a level of self-hate
I can't come back from.
You've created a monster rooted so deep within,
This is your outcome.

If this is how it will always be,
then I don't care to be good anymore.
I'm angry and volatile,
I've accepted the traumas don't have any cure.

So, I will be exactly who you want me to be,
I will cause destruction wherever I go.
I've stopped caring, no one can control me,
You've created a monster, just so you know.

disposable

What hurts the most isn't what you did.
But how you acted like you didn't do anything.
How you would blame me for being broken and messed up,
And not take accountability for everything.

You used me
Like I was nothing,
Like you owned me,
And reminded me everyday
how disposable I was.

You broke down every part of me,
till there was nothing,
And then threw me out in the dirt ... because?

What was the reason?
What messed you up so bad
that you thought this was normal?
Where did this hatred for me stem from?
What is it about me that's so incredibly awful
It justifies treating me this way?
Sometimes this world seems so dark
I question whether I should stay.
At this point I've seen so much,
I no longer hope to see a better day.

stay

I want you to see me standing before you
as I am and accept it.
At one point you chose me,
but I'm starting to feel like you regret it.

I don't want you to glance but truly look at me, and
    say those three words like you mean it.
I look for desire and longing in your eyes, and
    it breaks my heart when I can't see it.

I want you to hold me so tight that
I never question if I'm worthy of your love.
Reassure me I have something in me
that's worth staying for.
Put effort into this relationship
without me having to ask for it,
Without making me
feel like it's a chore.

I wish I didn't have to entertain
　　　in order for you to listen.
Dress up for you
　　　to look my way.
Work tirelessly
　　　for you to notice.
Fight for you to hear
　　　what I have to say.

　　　I wish I didn't have to beg
for you to love me.
　　　I wish me simply being here
was enough.
　　　　　　　I wish it didn't hurt this much to love you.
　　　　　　　I wish you weren't so quick to give up.

where did you go?

I look at you now and no longer recognise you.
The person I used to know is gone.
I'm no longer able to get close because
you make me feel like I don't belong.

I feel like I'm grieving for a person I've lost,
while you're stood right in front of me.
I feel so disconnected and distant around you,
when I search in your eyes I no longer see
The person I used to know.

I'm at a loss,
where did that person go?

past friend

Sometimes friendships aren't for life,
They're for seasons,
And if it no longer serves you then let it go,
Whatever the reason.

Sometimes us humans grow apart,
Through no fault of our own.
We have to accept the pieces no longer fit,
And that we have grown.

Doesn't make the friendship
any less meaningful,
The friendship served its purpose
and now it's come to an end.
You can hold on to all the great memories
for the rest of your life,
And remember all the lessons you've learned
from your past friend.

sorry they got caught

If you have to
   ask for an apology
then they're not
   really sorry,

they're just sorry
they got caught.

If you have to explain
what they did wrong
and fight for your closure,

then it's a losing battle
not worth being fought.

deserve better

Whether you believe it right now or not,
you deserve better.

You deserve someone who thinks
you're great.

Find someone who
respects you for you,
and spare yourself
the heartache.

goodbye

At first it hurt,
but it doesn't anymore.
Most days I forget,
I no longer feel sore.
And then I feel guilty,
does that mean I don't care?
If I saw you now,
I wouldn't run up to you,
I would just stare.
I'd be too cautious to get close
because the person I once knew
is no longer there.

I grieved that person a long time ago,
They only exist in my memory.
Who I knew, what I thought was real –
Turns out, it wasn't reality.

I'm not angry or sad,
I'm indifferent.
I just want you to be at peace.
And even though we no longer speak,
I just hope you finally
feel free.

Sometimes it feels easier to stay quiet,
It feels safer that way.
We continue living our separate lives,
There's so much we don't say.
But if you ever come across this
I just want you to know,

I hope you're doing okay.

IT'S NOT FINE

(struggles / hitting a new low)

'it's fine.'

I like to sleep in the day,
And stay up at night.
Because it's the only time I'm left alone,
And not made to feel guilty about life.

'it's fine.'

I'm exhausted,
Tired of constantly being in survival mode.
Feels like I've been stuck here my whole life,
And there's no end to this road.

'it's fine.'

I've spent the past seven years
    working towards a future I never chose.
And now my days are cursed with regret.
I'm in too deep that I'm scared to admit,
I'm living an existence I'd rather forget.

'it's fine.'

I'm finding it difficult to come to terms with the fact,
That the person I see in the mirror
    isn't who I am or want to be.
And it terrifies me to think about how
My true self might never be allowed out or set free.

'it's fine.'

I feel like I'm running out of time,
And I haven't achieved anything yet.
The clock is ticking and everyone's watching,
By now I should have had my life all set.

'it's fine.'

I'm tired of empty conversations,
Meaningless small talk that leads to nothing.
I'm desperately craving something real,
I just want to feel something.

'it's fine.'

I find it hard to truly let people in,
So I create versions of myself people like to see.
I've played charades my whole life,
So I no longer know what it means to be me.

'it's fine.'

I'm scared of being judged,
So I've learned to put on a mask.
I wish people were forgiving and compassionate,
Why does that feel like such a big ask?

'it's fine.'

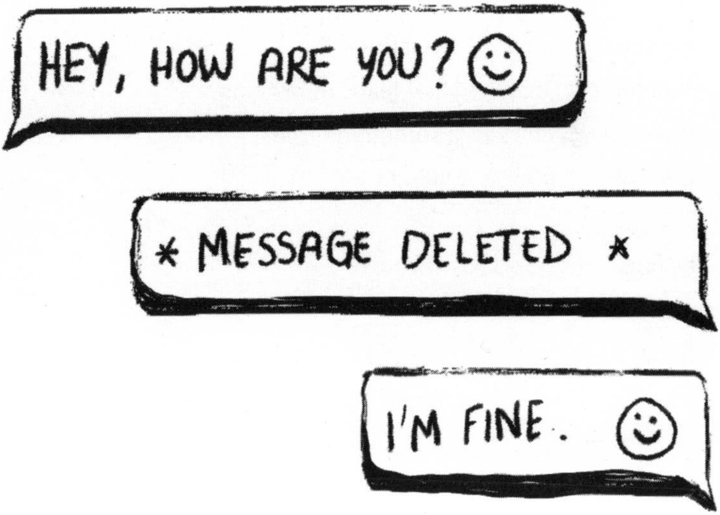
HEY, HOW ARE YOU?
* MESSAGE DELETED *
I'M FINE.

i don't want to be strong

I don't want to be strong.
I don't want to fight.
I just want to feel safe,
And *trust* things will be alright.

i'm not okay

For as long as I can remember
I've always had this void in my life,
It's this empty feeling deep deep inside of you
that you can't quite shake –
no matter how hard you try.
It sort of consumes and eats away at you,
You'll have great happy moments
and just when you thought everything was fine
– surprise!
The feeling always comes back,
it's just a matter of time.

The constant frustration to fill this void,
something to ease the pain.
What's the cause?
Nobody knows.
Yet you feel the same sad, hollow feeling
every single day.
It leaves me feeling so empty and down,
like I'm missing something somehow.
Something that's a big part of me
and once I have it,
I'll be happy.

I just need that one thing,
this missing key,
and when I get my hands on it,
I'll be complete.

I've tried everything – friends, education, material stuff,
    but no matter how hard I try,
it never seems to be enough.
It sucks,
and I know people will say
that you just need to be positive,
or the solution to all of your problems is self-love.
But it's not as simple as that,
not when you've got to the point
where you just feel numb.

I thought that when I grew up
things would be different,
I just thought ...
it would be different.

You look at other people
and they always look so happy.
You know you observe people's lives
whether that be in person, social media, TV,
and it seems to come to them so naturally.
And I know all of that stuff can be misleading,
    but when you feel so down and empty,
you can't help but think, *why can't that be me?*

Because you want **that**,
you so desperately want **that**,
and you feel like you're doing the right things,
you're having fun with your friends,
having late-night chats,
dancing to silly music,
and in the moment it feels great,
you're in a good, happy place,
but that happy feeling always goes away.
And the sad emptiness kicks in again.

Do I sound crazy?
                        God, I think I sound so crazy.

These thoughts tend to hit me
late at night,
And that's when I write.
Sometimes I'm so overcome
with emotion
that I just cry,

and I don't know why.
Makes me feel like
there's something wrong with me,
It's so sad to admit, that it becomes easier to lie
and act like everything's fine.

So that's what I say,
I say I'm fine.

Events from my past affect my adult life,
I lash out, feel down out of nowhere
and I can't explain why.
It just gets so messed up in my head sometimes
and there's no way to escape it,
Not when it's all happening in your mind.
And so you just beat yourself up

                    and beat yourself up
Until you feel so small,

               you know,
you can be in a room full of people
and still feel so   alone.

I can put on an act
and pretend that I'm tough,
but deep down I never quite
feel brave enough.
Sometimes I feel so small
in this big world,
And all I have are my words

to keep my sense of control.
One day, I'll look back
and it won't hurt anymore,
I'll be able to look back at what happened
and not feel so sore
Because there's no cure.

No way to fix it,
it's just something
you learn to live with,
But it'll get easier,
of that I'm sure.

You are not   the demons in your mind,
You are not   the hurt and pain you feel inside,
You're stronger than that,   you can fight.

Understand that it's all temporary
and that these things take time.

So chin up,
breathe,
allow yourself to feel everything there is to feel,
You're going to get through this,
Give it some time
                            and you'll heal.

anxiety

I'm a prisoner in my own mind.
                    It keeps telling me I'm shit,
                    a waste of space,
                    fucking up my life.

I sit here feeling sorry for myself,
knowing
          full
              well
                  that as
                      each day
                          goes by,
                              the less
                                  opportunity
                                      I have.

It's a daily reminder that I'm running out of time.
These are the thoughts that burden my mind,
keep me up at night, make me realise
that however hard I try
I am not fine.

I'm tired.

Tired of pretending and living this lie.
I'm not alright and I haven't been for a while.

I'm sick to death of feeling sad,
walking around with a heavy heart,
forcing all of my energy into just being okay,
when I'm not.

I'm weak, emotional, fragile.
I put up a strong game face.
But all you need to do is ask me the right questions
and it'll all come pouring out.

   The dark thoughts,
                    anxiety,
                              self-doubt

How sometimes I just need
to sit in a room by myself,
to calm the thoughts in my head
down.

Because you see, on the outside
everything is still, everything feels normal,
but up
          in here,
          in my mind,
it is so fucking loud.
I feel everything at once,
it's killing me,
I'm losing my mind.

Tell me, how do I escape?
When my worst demons are on the inside.
I'm buried alive.

In the endless battle
between my life and my mind,
it's time for me to admit
that I'm losing this fight.
I'm watching my personality
slowly die,
I'm giving in to it,
I'm surrendering to anxiety's side.

I just
want it
to
stop.

But it
won't
it never
stops.

It controls you, eats you up,
makes you believe
that it's all your fault.

depression

It's not that I don't want to be happy.
It's that despite my best efforts I can't bring myself to be
happy.

I feel suffocated, embarrassed, ashamed.
Why did I have to be this way?
I have a great family, amazing friends, good academic results –
On paper everything is okay
Yet all I ever seem to see is sadness and grey.

It's like there's this constant burden on you
pulling you to the ground,
and however hard you try you can't haul yourself out.
You can't bring yourself to care,
   about anything, not me,
      not him,
         not her.

Living has become a constant nightmare.
And it's just not fair.

They will tell you to *try yoga, go for a walk, listen to meditation.*
Have you tried exercising daily and going on medication?
It's a disease that affects every aspect of my life,
my relationships, my work, my education.

And even to this day, despite my best efforts to explain,
I am met with blind hesitation.

They ask me *why are you always sad?*
I tell them I don't know ...
                    I don't know.

What I do know is that I wake up every morning feeling like
    absolute shit
and that that's become my norm.

I'm afraid of the outside world,
                    afraid of putting my guard down
In fear that I will be judged for
                    something I cannot control.

Where's the fairness of it all?
Do you think I enjoy watching myself fall
into this hole of self-hate, shame and loathing?
So, I just hide and put up a wall that's so high,
    you will never see my pain or any of my flaws.
I create this character and she is perfect, invincible.

I live these two different lives, one for the public
and one just for me late at night.
Because that's easier than admitting you have a problem ...
                    and that's the problem.

The stigma is real, people.
And it will not go away until we realise
that mental health *is* a big deal.

It's the hidden disease affecting so many lives.
Wake up and listen to the silent cries.
It's the kid that never speaks
                         or the guy who's always tired,
The woman who's too emotional
                         or that man who just got fired
because he was absent
A lot.
He couldn't get out of bed due to his mental health.
But do you think any of his colleagues knew that?
Of course not.

Depression is the hell inside of me that swallows me up daily.

suicide

We just stood
> there,
in shock as we looked
> down,
so many questions running through our head.

Wondering if we had just done something,
> anything,
then maybe things could've turned out different.

At the age of just four his mother told him he was a mistake.
  Said that if she had it her way, he wouldn't be here today.
She resented him, despised him, blamed him for everything,
Couldn't look him in the eyes without being filled with rage.

She would tell him that he was the reason his dad walked out,
the day she knew she was pregnant everything changed.
She went from being madly in love,
  getting high, drunk every night,
to juggling two jobs and struggling to pay rent.
Now she's 'a single mum with no future' and
of course he's the one to blame,
and she reminded him of this every single day.

By age 11 he'd seen it all –
drug addiction, violence, sexual abuse.
He tried to shut it all out as best he could,
but no matter how hard he'd try, it was no good.
Because the problems kept growing
and just when he thought he'd seen enough –
he'd entered high school.
Under the false impression this was a fresh start,
to finally be himself, who knew kids could be so cruel?
They beat him, shamed him, spat on his food.
Mocked him, chased him, but somehow he made it through.
He was no longer living at this point, just struggling to survive,
but with no one to turn to,
what else could he do?

Wasn't long until the teachers labelled him a problem child.
Said he was disruptive, an inconvenience,
If he didn't settle down he'd be kicked out.
Didn't even try to understand him.
He wanted to push the bad stuff all out, but how?
He couldn't fight it anymore, he'd put up with it for too long,
    He no longer cared, he was getting angry now.

Problems at school, the streets, at home,
where the fuck was he supposed to go?

By this point his emotions took over,
he was angry, violent, abusive
he'd completely lost control.
He was done caring about anything,
he didn't give a shit anymore.

By age 16 he was walking in his father's footsteps,
lost and consumed by self-hate.
Took drugs to block out the thoughts in his head,
anything to numb the pain.
Desperately wanting to get away, escape to a better place,
a place where he could call home, a place where he felt safe
To face another day,
but that doesn't happen in the real world.
See, there is no light at the end of the tunnel,
not for people in this place.

He wasn't a bad kid, he was just scared.
Left to fight this world on his own.
Desperately wanting someone to care.
Wasn't long until he gave in to it,
he became someone he hates.
No longer wanting to fight it anymore,
he'd accepted this was his fate.

And just like that he ended it.
   No words,
        no note.

Didn't even make it to his 18th birthday.
Sad thing is, given the chance,
he could've been great.
But none of that matters now
because it's too late.
He can no longer be saved,
brought back from the grave
to live another day.

We live in a world where young kids
turn to suicide as an escape.
A way to finally feel free, because living has
become their biggest source of pain.

Why do we never realise our mistakes?
Why do we only learn when it's too late?
Local news will report this incident as just another case,
come up with excuses like he wasn't mentally sane
or how kids are so easily influenced these days.
Give it a few days and you won't even remember his name.
Just another statistic – and so many people
    go the exact same way.
This is the world in which we live.

It's such a cruel world,
it's such a shame.

not angry, just in pain

They were labelled the troubled kid.
The one with anger issues.
That destroyed everything that came near it.
That you can't help but wish you

                Had never met.

But what if you knew about
all the actions the kid regrets?
How they lash out in the moment but later forget

                Why they even behaved that way?

That they can't help how they act
and no matter how hard they try,
they can't make their behaviour change.

If only you knew that they weren't an angry kid,
they were just in pain.

'too much'

I've always felt like a burden,
always been made to feel like I was 'too much'.
Too emotional,
               too sensitive,
                                  too dramatic,
no matter how much I hide or suppress,
it was never enough.

strong woman

I don't want to be a 'strong woman'.
I don't want to prove I can continuously
rise back after every test life throws at me.
I don't want to have my guard up and fight through life.
I just want to feel safe enough to be *carefree*.

am i the bad guy?

Am I the bad guy?
Sometimes anger consumes me
And the rage takes over,
I do things a good human shouldn't do.
Once the anger calms down
and the guilt washes over,
I'm reminded that no matter how hard
I work on myself, I can't hide the truth.

The pain has rooted so deep,
it's found a home inside me.
It grows every day
and seeps through my veins,
Once I've pushed everyone away
it'll be too late.
Guilt and shame the only
things that remain.

Is it my fault?

Am I the bad guy?

I beat myself up over
everything that's happened,
Look at how life's turned out
and ask myself

Why?

Why me?

And I'm angry
because I'm stuck
with a life I didn't choose.
Thanks to someone else's mistakes
I'm collateral damage,
And these dark thoughts
Are getting harder to manage.

Left to pick up the pieces with no instructions,
One wrong step and I've hit self-destruction.
Trying my best to play pretend and fit in.
But after years of trying, it's finally kicked in.

I don't fit this world of normal people with their normal lives.
Who can go through the mundane activities
and shut off their mind.
No trauma,
no guilt,
no resentment,
no hate,
Starting to lose hope it will be better,
Perhaps this is my fate.

How is it that you did all the damage
but I have to live with the pain?
And despite my best efforts
I can't make these feelings
Go away.
Thanks to you I'll never know
what it's like to live a normal day.
Was it worth it?
What did you really gain?

All of this because of someone else's mistake.
Saying sorry doesn't make this feeling go away.
I'm scared to admit this cycle is hard to break.

Maybe this is my fate.

guilty

Sometimes I feel so guilty
for feeling the way I do,
Even though I understand
That you can't choose
The cards you've been dealt.
This is just the way life is.
I just wish this wasn't how I felt.

I didn't ask to be this way,
And sometimes I worry these feelings will always stay,
And no matter how much I repress and try to shut
them
out,
they'll never go away.

Sometimes I ask myself *why me*? This all feels so painfully unfair.
I wish I knew what it felt like to be blissfully ignorant,
To have the privilege to not care.

I can't stay but I also can't walk away,
So what do I do?
I just want these thoughts to stop,
I just want to make it through.

angry

You're human, and that's okay.

You're complex,
you're hurting and
you're in pain.

Sometimes the pressure to contain it all becomes too much
And it bursts out in anger.

You say things
                    you later regret.
You act in a way
                    you no longer recognise,
You do things
                    you wish to forget.

We're human. We make mistakes.
I'd rather be real and show you my truth
        than live a life that's fake.

I can't put on a smile and act like everything's okay
Because truth be told,
I don't think I have what it takes.

The anger inside has taken its toll.
It's rooted deep within me and
filled my soul.

home

I put on a tough exterior,
I build myself up to be brave.
Strong enough to handle
anything life throws at me,
But, you know what it is I really crave?

To know what it feels like to be home.
To exist and not be so alone.
To belong and feel understood.
To feel loved and wanted like a human should.

I want to feel seen
without having to ask for it.
I want to let down my guard
without fear of being judged.
I want you to tell me
it's going to be okay
and that this is a safe space.
Tell me, is that
asking for too much?

I'm walking on egg shells.
In constant survival mode.
I just want to let go of all this built-up tension,
Lay my head down in peace.

I've never really known
what it feels like to be home,
And now it feels too late,
I'm all grown.

tired

I'm so tired.
>Every day feels the same and it's getting harder to escape.
>I'm starting to feel numb.
>I'm struggling to convince my brain of better days.

>No one around here understands me,

I'm tired
>Of forcing myself to fit in.
>My whole life feels like a lie,
>And I'm finally letting the reality sink in.

>I'm working towards something I don't want,
>To please people I don't like.
>I'm trying so hard to be a version of myself I know I'm not,
>And it feels like I'm in too deep to make things right.

>I try to do little things to make me happy,
>But none of it makes the pain go away.
>Have I just wasted my life?

I'm tired
>Of trying to convince myself I'm okay.

complain

Too many of us live to escape.
Spend our working time
counting down the days.
When we talk about our lives
we always complain.
Why have we accepted life has
to be this way?

break the cycle

How can I sleep peacefully
When I know about the evil that breeds within me?
I can try to change as much as I want
but I'm still cut from the same cloth.
I can see my life going up in flames
and yet I'm drawn to it like a moth.

There's no escaping this hell.
There's no breaking the cycle.
Maybe I should just give up?
Because I'm tired of living
A life rooted in survival.

I don't want to be a fighter.
I don't want to be strong.
I just want to be normal,
I just want to feel like I belong.

i want to feel something

I want to feel something.
I want to believe life is worth living for.
All I see is the same old life on constant repeat.
And I refuse to believe this is all there is,
there has to be more.

survivor

People call you a survivor like it's something heroic.
But that is far from the truth.
It is not a choice but misfortune,
To be stripped of innocent youth.

It's being constantly vigilant,
and scraping through existence just to live another day.
It is not strong nor powerful,
It is living in constant fear and suffocating pain.

I didn't choose to be this way,
It's a life that was forced onto me.
The person I could've been was taken away.
And that's something I'm reminded of constantly.

are you okay?

I was having a really rough day,
When a complete stranger
came up to me and
asked me if I was okay.
For some reason I was speechless,
I didn't know what to say.

Usually when someone asks you
hey you okay?
it feels like nothing.
You know, you just respond
yeah I'm fine,   or something.

People ask the question
with no real interest,   which is fine.
I understand it's a casual conversation starter,
a way to be polite.

But this time was different.
The way she said

                        are you okay?
it came out of nowhere.

Her voice was sincere.
When she looked at me she didn't stare –
She looked deep into my eyes and

saw straight through me.
I knew in that moment she saw parts of me
I don't let anyone see –
The vulnerable,   the sad,   the lonely.
And I could see her shift herself ready to console me.

I can't really describe how I felt,
A mix of betrayal and relief.
I could feel my walls crashing down.
I was caught off guard, confused in disbelief.

Even though a part of me wanted to let go,
I chose to stay quiet.
I clenched my teeth, squeezed the tears in my eyes
whilst the emotions inside me went riot.

For some reason I wasn't ready to open up
However, what she said and did next
will stay with me forever.

She said *I don't know what you're going through,*
And I may never understand.
We don't need to talk about it,
But in this moment, let's just hold hands.

And that's exactly what we did, and it changed everything.
In a world that asks so much from you,
she didn't want anything.
In a world where you can feel so empty and alone
Her reaching out meant something.

I never did tell her how I felt,
Mostly because I never understood it myself to explain.
But I don't think it mattered,
Because somehow without saying anything
I felt like she understood my pain.

And that was enough to get me through that day.
I guess the lesson here is,
If you sense something may not be right
Ask that person if they're okay.

They may not tell you the truth
But pay attention to what they do or do not say
Because you might hear it anyway

Without realising it,
that woman saved my life that day.

i see you

I see you.
The pain and sadness
behind your forced smile.
How you've become quieter,
And haven't been yourself in a long while.

You're so fragile,
One question away from falling apart.
I know you think nothing can heal your pain,
But when I see you, I see your heart.

I know you think so little of yourself.
But to me, you're the strongest person I know.
Despite everything life's thrown at you,
you choose to keep fighting.
Your strength comes from
all the things you don't dare to show.

TO MY YOUNGER SELF...

(early years)

to my younger self

My younger self is
my biggest motivation in life.
I work hard to make something of myself
to make her proud.
I break boundaries and push myself
so she can see a better world.
A world where there's no doubt
She can be whoever she wants to be.
A world where she feels understood,
accepted and at peace.

Because right now she's scared,
Her days feel dark, lifeless,
and she doesn't see a way out.
Her hope is slowly disintegrating
and clouded by crippling self doubt.
Her light is fading.
And she's contemplating
giving up.
Settling on life because
no amount of fighting will ever be enough.

I work hard so
she never doubts her choices again.
Make her realise
there's nothing in this world she cannot attain.
I want to show her
all the things she goes on to achieve
like a child shows their mother.
I want her to see her worth,
so she never compares herself to another.

I want to see her eyes light up with all the wild possibilities,
No longer afraid but excited by the boundless opportunities.
I want to watch her face glow with hope,
Knowing she doesn't need to sacrifice who she is to fit in.
That she can be the hero of her own story.
Rather than live a life someone else has written.

I want to be someone younger me aspires to be.
Someone who makes her feel loved and understood.
Gives her strength and confidence,
And changes her 'can'ts' to 'maybe I could?'

I want to be the person I needed back then.
I want to be the hero in her eyes.
I want to tell her

> 'it's going to be okay ...
> Be brave and shoot for   the skies.'

losing your innocence

At some point in life you lose your innocence.
You lose that innate childlike wonder.
Your smile gets a lot smaller.
And it becomes harder to connect
to how you felt when you were younger.

Some lose it earlier than others,
Their environment strips their innocence away,
It conditions them to grow up and resets their mind,
Trains them to think a different way.
Once the innocence is lost,
it's almost impossible to regain.
You can't seek comfort in it anymore
because you're too traumatised by the pain.

Some spend a lifetime
seeking the feeling again,
But sadly the light inside fades.
The glimmer of hope and imagination
loses its spark and you're left
with the life you have made.

boundaries

Something I wish we were taught as children
is the importance of boundaries.
Instead we're told to give ourselves away
for people to judge.
We think it's selfish
to put our needs first,
So we people please and
wonder why we never feel enough.

I never had boundaries growing up.
I never learned to stand up for myself and say *no*.
I just did whatever people asked of me,
And it ruined me mentally as I couldn't grow.

Which is why I now want to reclaim my power,
I want to build boundaries to protect myself.
I want to be the one in control of my life,
I will no longer neglect my happiness and mental health.

It is not selfish to have boundaries.
It does not make me a bad person
to put my needs first.
It is both necessary and empowering.
I've learned my lesson the hard way,
I will no longer let myself get hurt.

inner child

I look in the mirror now,
And I see someone who's a lot calmer.
Not so quick to pick herself apart,
But rather doesn't want anyone to harm her.

Now when I see myself,
I stand and gaze.
I see the strength and growth,
How I managed to get out of the dark phase.

I see someone who's been through a lot,
and made it to the other side.
I see someone who's worked hard on themselves,
and it fills me with pride.

I see someone I love and care about deeply.
I'll never allow myself to hurt me again.
I will be patient and I'll listen,
And learn to be my own friend.

I'll be attentive to your needs,
I'll do my best to protect you.
I'll hold your hand through it all,
I'll be by your side to see it through.

I won't hurt you anymore,
Because you honestly deserve the world.
I'm here for you whenever you need me,
You deserve to be happy, little girl.

human

I want to apologise to my younger self,
She didn't deserve all the pain she got, she deserved love.
And I'm ashamed that I couldn't give that to her,
I wasn't strong enough to rise above
The hate and the pain.
Instead of being there for myself
I was consumed by shame.

But I now realise she wasn't weak, angry or a bad kid.
She was a survivor
and the strongest person I know to get through what she did.

She's managed to make a life for herself.
It's been difficult but a blessing to watch you grow.
I didn't say it at the time but I'm really proud of you,
It's just something I wanted you to know.

Looking back now,
It's clear that you saved my life.
You pushed me to become the person I am today,
When you had no one by your side,
You chose to stand up for what's right.

So much pain goes unspoken,
And ignoring it all only leaves you more broken.
It's time to make peace with myself and heal,
Allow myself to take the mask off and show what's real.
I no longer desire to be what others expect me to be,
I want to allow myself to be human and finally set me free.
I'm tired of playing pretend, I just want to be me.

I want to finally give you the peace you deserve,
I want to tell you it's okay.
I know you're not perfect,
but that doesn't make you a bad person,
It just means you're human and you're in pain.
And beating yourself up and hating on yourself,
Will never make that pain go away.

From this day forward
I choose to protect and take care of myself.
I will be my biggest cheerleader,
I will hold my hand through all the darkness and pain.
I will not abandon myself when things get tough,
no matter how bad things get I will choose to stay.

Because I am worthy of love,
I deserve to be happy from within,
I choose to appreciate my mind and my thoughts,
And accept the skin that I'm in.

I am all I have,
I will learn to be my own friend.
I will stick it out through thick and thin.
It's just me and myself till the end.

It's uncomfortable talking about this,
And honestly, I don't know if I want to open up.
Talking about this isn't easy for me,
it's painful,
it's tough.
But I just remember how alone my younger self felt,
And if this can help just one person,
then that's more than enough.

AM I ENOUGH?

(expectations / pressures)

existential crisis

I spend most of my time avoiding   people.

More specifically, avoiding   the questions
they will inevitably ask.

Like, *what are your plans for the future?*
Have you got a job yet?
Where do you see yourself in ten years' time?
I wish I could answer them,
come up with something grand and impressive.
But I can't.

So instead I just sit in my room all day,
hide away from the world,
steeped in self doubt.
Wondering how much longer I can get away with saying
I'm just figuring myself out.
Because eventually people will get tired of hearing that,
and they'll come hitting at me much harder,
telling me that I don't have the time,
I'm wasting away my future and that
if I want to get anywhere in life,
I need to make the decision **now**.
Everything has to be decided **now**.

But the thing is I'm not ready **now**.
And the thought of making a forced decision
that I'll regret my entire life
absolutely terrifies me.

It's as if as soon as you hit your twenties you become
    overwhelmed by everything.
Everything you've been taught,
                        the people around you,
                                the pressure from society.

You start to overanalyse all of it,
And suddenly it hits you **now** – unbearable, debilitating anxiety.
You find yourself staying awake at night,
the uncertainty of your future
haunts you in your sleep.
The pressure keeps growing and growing,
it becomes difficult
to breathe.
You hide yourself away,
too ashamed to speak
because you don't know what
you're doing with your life,
and you're too scared
to face reality.

Reality these days is filled with
   restrictions, limitations, set criteria.
It's like **now** I'm forever facing this big black wall,
living in this constant state of fear.
Fear that everyone else will move on with their life,
do Great Amazing Things, whilst you're just left Behind.
You're just
here.

Sat in this empty room, feeling like such a pathetic failure.
It's been months, I told myself I would've figured it out by **now**,
but things are not getting clearer,
It's been months **now**, I thought I'd be a lot happier.

Once you hit your twenties everything changes.
You can no longer enjoy yourself because
What once made you happy,
now makes you feel guilty.

Every waking day is a reminder that
you're taking time away from the person you should be.
A contributing member of society
Earning a respectable amount of money.
People keep telling me what to do,
apply here,
enter this programme,

sign up for this. It's all too much,

                    just back

                            off, please

                  just let me

                                breathe.

Your expectations and pressures are suffocating.
I know it's my future and that I'm running out of time –
but please try to understand –
    I'm just not ready **now**.
I worry I never will be.

It's funny how everyone seems to know what they want for
    my life.
Everyone except me.

expectations

Expectations will be the death of me.
From day one we are told
What is expected of us.

Conform, go to school, get the grades.
You have to be the best,
no room to screw up.

We put our fate in the control of others
and wait to be judged.
Define ourselves by grades and numbers,
forever believing that we're not good enough
because our actions do not match our expectations.

What is expected of us is to know what to do
for the rest of our lives at just sixteen,
despite up until that point having no real life experiences.

I mean how could we?
At what point were we given the opportunity
To grow as individuals, discover ourselves, live free from scrutiny

From day one it is drilled into our heads that
Our main goal in life is stability and financial security.
Anything else is time wasted.
Teachers tell us if you want success in this life then
you need to go to university.

It doesn't matter if it doesn't feel right, right now.
Because once you've graduated things will become clear.
Six years on and I find myself still here.

Thoughts about my future terrify me,
I can't sleep,
or eat.

It's the reason why my dark thoughts are keeping me up
at night, spiralling my anxiety.
Because I don't have a five-year plan,
and for some reason that makes me feel guilty.

See, my biggest fear in life is to settle.
Just the thought of it haunts me in my sleep.
I've seen too many people give up,
live a life full of regrets.
And I don't want that
to be me.

To choose stability over your dreams is to let society win.
And I can't do that, I'm sorry.

Get a nine-to-five. Buy a house.
Get married before 30.
Work. Eat. Sleep. Repeat.
The average twenty-first-century daily routine.

No passion or drive,
We're just living machines
Whose only motivation in life
is making enough money.

Ask yourself –
Are you living or merely existing?

I'm 22 yet I fear I know
very little about 'real stuff'.
Like what the world looks like on the other side
or how it feels to be in love.

To settle now would be to give up on discovering
who I really am, I want to learn and explore.
If I don't get lost now,
how will I ever grow?
And maybe I am wasting time
But I have to take that chance,
I need to know for sure.

I'm sorry, but I cannot be what you want me to be,
Because to do that would mean sacrificing everything
that makes me
me,
and settling for a life where
I'll never truly be happy.

I've spent my whole life
trying to please others.
It gets tiring and lonely,
I am calm on the outside,
but on the inside I am screaming.

See, despite my best efforts,
I am clueless when it comes to my life.
My gut tells me that the path you've got in mind
Isn't right – at least not for me.
My life should not be dictated by a degree
I chose to do when I was sixteen,
because everyone I knew told me
the right thing was university.
I look back now and I can't help but disagree.

The truth is, I have so many ambitions and dreams,
I want to change the world, spread love and positivity.

But I fear soon I will have to face this harsh reality.
The doubts in my head will take over
And the passion inside will die.
I'll surrender to society's pressure
And settle for a comfortable life.

One with
No passion
No hopes
No desires.

Just the same old routine,
Never to know what it feels like,
To really be in love with my life.

don't ask me what I'm doing with my life

Please don't ask me what I'm doing with my life,
'cause honestly, I don't know.
I am a ball of constant, crippling guilt,
A fragile walking mess who's trying really hard not to show –

How insecure I am.

How, despite all my achievements thus far, I don't know if I can
Make it, be successful, whatever that even means.

I worry I will be a disappointment,
And my life isn't what it seems.

I feel this immense pressure to have my life figured out,
And yet, I have no idea where to start?
I should have a career, house and family by now,
And feel guilty to admit that's not what I want in my heart
– At least not now.
But time is running out.
This imaginary race beating inside me
says I have to keep up somehow.

What makes it worse is when I look around,
Everyone seems to have it figured out and I'm just like how?!
It's getting harder to be honest now.

So, I wrap my words in a lie,
To make it easier to hide how I really feel inside.
Making up a story that fits in with
your narrative for me,
Knowing that you'll never feel or see
what I have to be.

I don't know, man, I don't know.
And the part that really sucks is
I can't show you how I feel.
It's like we're not allowed to be broken, a mess,
Like the world can't handle what's real.

What's real is, I feel like a failure.
And I know I should be strong
And be a fighter,
But sometimes I question
If I can be my own saviour.

What if I'm not great?
What if I'm not good enough?
Having to deal with that realisation can be really tough.

I just wish something could come along and
pick me up from this dump.
But instead I just get expectations thrown at me,
and tough love.
So I hide how I feel and it's getting harder to
open up.

So, to answer your question,
I don't know what I'm doing and
I don't know if I'm good enough.

survival mode

The sad realisation that I've never really lived,   only survived.
The sudden awakening to the peaceful life I've been deprived.

Life is a constant race,
I'm doing the most just to
stop myself from drowning.
Just trying to get through the day,
But when I look ahead
all I see is a steep mountain.

Life expects results,
And it will throw you aside
if you don't meet its expectations.
I feel like I'm rushing through life,
going through every obstacle,
Yet I can't see a destination.

I'm so mentally drained
I barely speak to anyone anymore,
The light inside is dying.
I have no sense of self or purpose,
It's hard to motivate myself
to keep on trying.

It feels like a luxury to exist,
when you've spent your whole life
trying to survive.
And what hurts the most is knowing,
I'm watching my life pass me by.

keep on grinding

I feel this constant need to be productive,
And if I'm not then I have failed myself.
I push myself to be on this constant grind,
And when I inevitably burn out,
I'm too ashamed to reach out for help.

I have this innate need to prove I'm independent.
That I'm capable of doing everything on my own.
I wear my skills like accolades,
To show people how much I've grown.

Life has become a race,
And I'm competing with everyone,
    I'm always doing the most yet it's never enough.
No matter what I do I can't keep up with anyone.

I don't know where this need to prove my worth comes from,
    I just know it's been instilled in me from a young age.
And it's so deeply ingrained in my psyche,
That I cannot view myself any other way.

I push myself to be bigger and better,
But the reality is, it's never enough,
I fail to acknowledge all the things I've achieved thus far,
When it comes to myself, I'm too tough.

I don't even know what it is I'm working towards,
Who am I trying to impress?
And when I start feeling low and the doubts kick in,
My instinct is to work harder and suppress.

I recognise this isn't healthy,
But it's also a toxic cycle I can't break.
I just want to be someone I can be proud of.
Even if that means my mental health's at stake.

life to begin

What, you have dreams?
Dreams to be a star?
Who are you kidding?
People around here
don't make it very far.

You're just going to be disappointed,
What makes you so special anyway?
What makes you think people
will care about what you have to say?
You'll never be anything,
Society has been set up
to not let people like us win.
If you leave now you're throwing your life away –

Or maybe,
I'm finally letting it begin.

it's hard to believe in myself

You never asked what did I want?
You never even tried to understand.
All I got was expectations,
But never a helping hand.
  I'm done.
I'm done giving in
to your ever-growing list of demands.
I may not know what I'm doing,
but at least I'm living according to my plan.

You don't get it, you don't see –
That none of this is easy for me.
Do you know how hard it is to believe in your dreams?
This isn't about money, fame or vanity,
I just want the privilege to exist and be.
I want to de-condition everything society has taught me
I needed to *be* to feel worthy.

Why is it that the hardest thing to be
is happy?
Why is it too much to want more?
We spend so much time settling and repressing how we feel,
And not enough time finding the cure.
We wait until it's too late,
And then live with regret.
But I can't do that, I'm sorry.
I can't live a life I want to forget.

I'm going to de-condition
everything I've been told to be.
I'm tired of hearing the 'truth'.
I'm very aware that I'm running out of time
And am no longer in my youth.

But what's the alternative in life?
Why is there so much pressure
to have everything figured out by 25?
Why do I feel guilty for wanting more?
Why do I feel like society is set one way
and I'm the flaw?

I've tried living by your rules
but these feelings are taking over.
I'm sorry, but I want something more.
I've tried to fight these feelings
but I can't suppress them anymore.
When it comes to how I feel
it's just not something I can ignore.

There comes a point where
you have to make a decision
between the life set up for you
and the one you envision.
It's not always a choice,
it's fuelled by ambition,
these are the cards,
this is what you've been given.

feeling trapped

I look around and all I see is empty people,
Going through their monotonous daily lives.
Yes, they're walking, breathing, moving
but when you look deeper,
they're all dead inside.
The more time goes by
The more we forget what it's like
to have passions, excitement, desires.

I'm scared I'm going to end up like everyone else
in this place and it's slowly driving me insane.

Silently going through my everyday tasks,
but on the inside I'm screaming to break out.
Tired of going to a job I hate,
Making small talk,
Pursuing empty dreams.
One day I'm going to break.
All we seem to do is the same exact,
mind-numbing thing day after day.

But how do I escape?
How do I fill this void inside me?
What's the answer?
Spend more,
Work more,
What do I need to attain?

We just live for temporary moments,
Little bits of happiness to ease our pain.
But soon as those moments are finished
the dark thoughts creep up on us again.

I mean who says there's only
one way of living anyway?
Sometimes I feel like no one else gets it,
it's like sure, you can dream – but don't dream too big
because you need to be realistic,
I look around and no one seems to be happy,
everyone's looking into their phone screens
to block themselves from reality
because reality has become too depressing.

We watch ourselves counting down the clock,
wasting time with our hollow lives?
Most people settle and just survive,
Scared to take a chance to know what it feels like to really be
    alive.
They tell me that this is the way to do things properly,
and I just can't help but question why.
Surely, I can't be wrong for wanting more in life?

One day I'll wake up and think fuck,
I've wasted my life away.
And you know what the worst part is?
I'll only have myself to blame.

I can't let myself become that person,
I refuse, I need to make a change,
Life isn't a movie, I can't just wait for things to
magically fall into place,
if I want to truly live, to make something of myself,
then the change has to start today.

what's next?

Growing up I was what most people would call a geek.
Straight-A students, who'd stress out over their grades
and dedicate most of their time to study.
Yep, that was me.

From a young age it was instilled into our brains
that if we want to make something of ourselves
then we need to go to university!
I mean it was practically a necessity.
Why? Because it would
increase your job prospects and
ensure financial stability,
And when you're sixteen that's the ultimate goal really ...

I remember being asked
Taz, what do you want to be?
I had no idea.
I wasn't thinking about my future,
I barely remembered the day of the week,
and I definitely did not deal well with responsibility.
The truth is I never knew the answer to that question,
I based my choices on my GCSEs
I did well at Law so I figured,
hey, a lawyer it shall be.

Studied hard,
Two years passed
and I finally started university.
It was anything but easy.
Reading lists were ever-growing,
stress was at an all-time peak.

Cram for the exam you have next week. It was crazy.
I'd love to tell you stories about how
I was having the time of my life
and going to crazy parties
but I can't really.

The truth is I spent most nights exhausted,
reading case law at a 24-hour library.
I was living the dream.
Three years later and I finally
got myself a bachelor's degree,
and that's when it hit me.
I came to the realisation
that this isn't who I want to be.

After graduation came the stress.
Filling in one job application after the other,
dreading the impending student loan debts,
I was a mess.

Struggling to get by
with only one question on my mind,

What's Next?

The next few months were hard,
Fill out an application form, get rejected,
and then inevitably fall apart.
Build myself back up and restart,
Felt like I had an empty future ahead of me
and I wasn't getting very far.

Stop. Reassess.
The anxiety hits me all over again.
Back to the drawing board, I guess.
Overwhelmed by the stress,
I confess, I don't know what's next.
And we're back to the first step.

Looking back now, hitting rock bottom was the
best thing that could've happened to me.
It took feeling like an absolute failure to finally set me free.
I had a fresh start,
a chance to rebuild myself
Be whoever I wanted to be.
Because what's there to lose when you have nothing?
But what's there to gain?

Everything.

I started writing, creating films,
performed spoken-word poetry,
discussed important topics and
talked about things that mattered to me,
I made people stop, think, feel.
For the first time in my life
I was doing something that felt real.

No more pressure to compete,
I simply worked hard doing what I love and told myself,
whatever will be will be.
I grew an online audience,
connected with people worldwide,
and for the first time in my life I saw things so clearly.
No longer adhering to social constructs,
I'm choosing my own path,
and I've never felt more free.

I want to feel, like *really* feel.
Travel the world and connect with people.
I want to help, make an impact,
tell incredible stories,
conquer all my darkest fears and live limitlessly.
No more running away anymore,
I want to delve into the unknown,
take risks and chances,
because as cliché as it sounds
we really do only live once,
and I don't plan on taking that for granted.

So ask me again *what's next?*
and I'll say the answer is easy.
What's next is continuing to work hard
doing what I love,
and an infinite amount of opportunity.

life's not fair

Let me guess,
The world's not fair
and it's against you.
Go on then,
give up like you always do,
mope around
feeling sorry for yourself.
What's the matter?
Can't handle the truth?

Would you like me
to sugar-coat it for you?
Tell you that everything's going to be fine
and come up with some easy excuse?
Well I'm not going to,
because life's not easy
and you're not a fool.

You keep acting like the victim all the time,
Constantly saying how things
aren't going your way when
the choice has always been
right there in front of you.

You've got the tools,
A working brain, a functioning body,
So, stop acting
like you haven't got a clue.

Yes, 'life's not fair',
and things aren't always going to go your way,
tell me something new.
I hate to break it to you,
but the world isn't going to be laid out nicely for you.

Every time things don't go right,
are you just going to sit around and wonder why?
Stay up late and cry yourself to sleep every night?
Is that really how you want to live your life?
Just become bitter and miserable?
Don't you ever get tired?
Tired of feeling so sorry for yourself?
When are you going to get it?
The world doesn't owe you anything, it never has,
So you need to get over this whole negative phase,
and leave all of that stuff in the past.

The biggest mistake is believing
that you don't have control over your life,
That it's not a choice,
when that couldn't be further from the truth.
If you want something,
you need to chase it,
The only person who can determine
your success in life, is you.

You don't like your job? Quit.
Don't see an opportunity? Create one.
Things aren't going to be handed to you on a plate,
you need to work hard for your craft,
you need to keep going until you get it done.
What you're going to learn is, life is complex,
You're gonna fail and get rejected
time and time again,
If it was easy, everyone would've already won.

Is it going to be hard?
Are you going to struggle?
Absolutely.

But don't let that stop you from
fighting for what could be a fantastic opportunity.
You're fighting for the chance
to be who you really want,
and that freedom right there,
is worth any amount of money.

So, stop saying you're going
to do something and actually do it.
At the end of the day,
something worth having never comes easy.
You can't keep playing the victim card your whole life.
Because next thing you know,
it'll all pass by in the blink of an eye,
You're sitting there in your death bed –
wondering why you've stopped yourself
from doing so many things in life.

There will be times when
you're gonna be stuck in jobs you hate,
be around people you don't like,
that's life.

And I'd be doing you an injustice to tell you otherwise.
It's not always going to be unicorns and butterflies,
It's gonna be hard work, determination
and in most cases sacrifice.
But what you need to do is decide
whether you're going to fight for what's right.

Trust me, I get it,
The world can at times
seem intimidating and scary,
but it can also be incredibly wonderful –
if you just let it be.

living out of fear

You live out of fear.
Because you're afraid of letting people down.
But if they truly care
and want the best for you,
Then they will come around.
And if they don't,
Then why does it matter?

What exactly are you trying to prove?

At some point you need
to let go if you want to live.
If your worth is conditional,
then there's only so much you can give
Before you lose yourself completely.
I understand stepping out
of your comfort zone isn't easy.
It's a path filled with guilt, doubt and pain.
Constantly having to reassure yourself
that it will be okay.

Putting yourself out there in a world so critical
Is terrifying and painfully difficult.
But if you give in to the fear,
you lose out on a life you chose.

A life that could turn out
in so many different ways,
but because of fear
you'll never know.

for anyone feeling lost in life

When I was 14,
I was too scared to dream.
I was a working-class kid with
immigrant parents and figured
those kinds of opportunities aren't
afforded to people like me.

So, I chose a path that was safe.
And it took 12 years of lying to myself
and graduating with a degree
to realise I had made a really big mistake.
This isn't what I wanted,
this isn't who I wanted to be.
And it was really hard to admit that
after all the hard work,
this didn't feel right to me.
And let me tell you, abandoning everything that you know
and worked so hard for
is scary.

But it did prove that no matter how hard you try,
you can't fight who you are.
Sure, you can play by the rules of society
and do as you're told
but it will only get you so far.
At some point you'll need to be honest with yourself
and when that day comes
you find yourself back at the start.

I went from having a five-year plan,
To feeling like a failure.
But I knew if I wanted to live a life I wanted,
there was no time for self-pity,
I needed to be my own saviour.

It's not easy to rebuild
and figure yourself out,
Especially when you're filled with
guilt, shame and self-doubt.
But it took hitting rock bottom to feel free,
Because when you take away all expectations
you finally get to be who you want to be.

You can't help who you are, what you like or dislike.
Society may have a path for you and
sometimes that path may not feel right.

At some point, you have got to decide.
Between living a life set out for you and
Living the one that you choose.
And it's a hard decision to make
but there's this huge freedom and happiness
that comes when you do.
I know it sounds super lame and cheesy,
but it's true.
Real happiness comes from
you being you.
It sounds so simple, right?
But for some reason
it's like, the hardest thing to do.

I still don't know what I'm doing with my life.
How or why I'm on this page.
But for anyone who needs to hear it,
I know it doesn't feel like it right now but
you do have the power to bring change.

Taking a chance is a risk,
You don't know how it's going to go,
But if you're never honest with yourself
and never push yourself forward,
How are you ever going to grow?

Sometimes life can feel too much and you lack self-love,
It feels like you're being pushed to a corner
and forced to give up.
But, when you feel defeated and helpless
that's when you need to rise above.
Truth is you are, and have always been, enough.

The answer doesn't come from anywhere else,
it comes from you,
So I'm going to ask you a question.
Between hiding and being your true self,
Which one do you choose?

HEALING

(growth / moving on / unlearning)

healing

People talk about healing like it's a peaceful process.
They don't talk about the guilt and pain
Of dissecting the trauma
And convincing yourself that
removing yourself from a toxic situation is okay.

They don't talk about the negative thoughts
that infiltrate your brain,
And manifest themselves in the most triggering ways.
You don't wake up and the pain just magically goes away,
Sadly, it doesn't work that way.

it's okay to be human

Something I wish I was taught growing up,
which would've prevented a lot of guilt and pain.
Is understanding that it's okay to be human,
That it's okay to make mistakes.

It's so damaging that we're taught
that we need to live to a certain standard,
And anything less than that is not enough.
Especially when those standards
have been proved to be unrealistic,
Causing stress, mental health issues
and a deep lack of self-love.

Living up to these unhealthy expectations
Inevitably led to resentment.
I started to hate who I was
and the life I lived,
But couldn't escape because I became
dependent on this way of thinking.
All this self-hate has been conditioned,
Now let that sink in.

I used to beat myself up for making mistakes.
I used to get frustrated
and live with anger and regret.
It was only when I started
to humanise myself
that I finally started to heal.
The weight disappeared
and my mind was finally reset.

grow

I
  want
    to
      strip
        it
        all

        aw
        ay,

        Ev
        er
        y
      thing
      I
know.

  I want to
      start afresh,
        Make my
          own choices
            on
            how
            I
            Grow.

it's okay to not be okay

Life gets hard sometimes.
There are days where I wake up
and I don't like what I see,
and it's not because of my looks,
it's as if I don't even like being me.

I get so frustrated at myself
that I take it out on others,
and then when I think about what I've done,
I feel so guilty –
because I know deep down
that person isn't me.

I look at how I've been living my life lately
and I haven't accomplished anything,
all I seem to do these days is work and sleep.
The same exact thing
every single week.

I try to be positive and keep it together,
but man, I am struggling.
It just feels so hard to be happy lately.
I haven't done the things I want to
because I just don't have the time,
and when I do, I feel so tired and exhausted
because I've been working crazy shifts every night.

And I worry that soon enough I'll lose confidence
and give up completely, settle and
become the person I never wanted to be.

Even as I'm saying this
all I keep thinking is
God, I sound so depressing.
It's only a matter of time
till people get bored and leave.
So I have to force every bit of my energy into
being super enthusiastic and happy
when that is so far from the reality.

The other night I came home from work
and I just completely broke down.
But I woke up the next day and carried on
living life as if everything was fine.
In the denial that if I keep repressing these thoughts,
somehow it'll get easier with time.

It won't.

It's sad because all people see
is what I show them on the outside.
They have no idea about all the hurt
and pain I hide.

How I cried myself to sleep
or the fact that I've been avoiding skyping my best friend,
because I don't want to show her this side.
The side where I just can't keep it together
and the most fucked-up part is that I have no idea why.
I feel both overwhelmed and empty
all at the same time.

It feels like people around here
don't make their dreams a reality,
they say life isn't fair or that they
were never given the opportunity.
And when you see that every single day,
you become disheartened,
you think that maybe your dreams are just that
– dreams.

But it's in that moment,
when you're the most down,
that's when you need to keep on going.

I know it sounds clichéd,
but I think sometimes we need to be reminded
that it's okay to not be okay.
Our biggest problem as a society
is that we don't communicate.
We'd rather pretend everything's fine
and suffer   silently.
Come home after a tough day
and break down   quietly.
If you're going through a tough time right now
and you are putting all of your energy
into just getting through another day,
know that I think you are incredibly brave.

Because I know how hard that shit is.

We'll be okay, in fact we'll be fucking great,
and one day we'll look back on this time
and be so proud of ourselves.
Thinking that we're glad we went
through the tough times because
it made us the person we are   today.

independent

I'm independent,
But it was never through choice.
There was no one to help guide me growing up,
So I had to find my own voice.

I spent years struggling and alone,
I so desperately wanted someone to hold my hand
and tell me it's going to be okay.
That they were there for me,
to listen and give advice.
And no matter how bad things got
they would always stay.

But that person never came.
So I learned to adapt to life alone.
I built myself up to take on every challenge,
went head first into the unknown.

And yes, I'm a stronger person because of it.
But I'm also guarded and comfortable alone.
I've learned to deal with everything myself,
I have become my own home.

true to myself

I want to live a life I can be proud of,
I want to look back and say I lived for me.
That I always stayed true to myself,
Despite the adversity.

But it isn't easy, living a life true to you
is a privilege not many people have.
At times it feels like a right you have to fight for.
I wasted so much of my life
giving so much of myself to other people,
but I don't have the energy to do that anymore.
All I know is,
I've only got one life.
So I intend on taking back my power
and living honestly,
If I'm to feel content in this lifetime,
then I have to make a promise to me,
that I will live life to the fullest.

I want to see my potential,
I want to live my best days.
I want to feel everything there is to feel.

No matter how tough it gets,
I need to be brave.
I'm going to be here for myself,
it's going to be okay.

night time

I feel the most myself at night time.
It's when I feel most safe.
Everyone's asleep, the world is silent,
And I can relax in my own space.

No one's around to judge,
I can exist guilt free.
I'm not constantly reminded of my failings.
I can get lost in my thoughts and breathe.
Somedays I sleep through the day
to stay up all night.
To avoid all the comments,
expectations and endless fights.
I'm tired, the kind of tired
no amount of sleep can fix.
The world feels like a scary place
and then you add all that pressure to the mix.

I just need time,
To heal and nurture my soul.
A chance to catch my breath and build myself up.
So I can mend myself whole.

humans break

Us humans,
we bruise
and we break.

We'll experience incredible highs
and emotional heartaches.

In your toughest moments,
when you're begging for the pain to go away,
be strong enough to get through another day.

Things will get better.
Take care of yourself.
Be kind and stay safe.

law of attraction

I was never taught to think for myself,
I was always told to act for others.
And it led to a miserable life.
Because I was working towards a life I didn't want,
I was too afraid of disappointing others
and not doing what's 'right'.

I was so beat down from the pressure and expectations,
That I began to grow cynical,
I was burnt out,
I couldn't see any other option,
And it was at the pinnacle

>Of my breakdown,
>That I was faced with a choice.
>I could continue living for others
>or I could listen to my inner voice.

I thought, *you know what?*
Just this once,
I'm going to do something for me.
I'm going to be brave enough
to envision the life I want.
Be courageous enough to speak it confidently.

I was bold with my ambitions and goals,
Because I figured I had nothing left to lose.
I wrote them all out and lived my life accordingly,
Because I was adamant on living a life I choose.
I never knew how much of an impact your mindset can have,
But I guess how my life turned out is the proof.

How you think and act
Sets the tone for the rest of your life.
You are in control of your own actions,
You get to decide what's wrong and right.

I did everything that was expected of me.
And fell into the trap of society,
But in the end the biggest lesson I learned,
Is that your focus determines your reality.

not my responsibility

I heard something the other day.
It opened my eyes
and finally made me see.
They said, 'what people think of you,
is not your responsibility'.

And it made me realise
how much unnecessary baggage I held onto,
I wear people's opinions of me
like weight on my shoulders.
I let them consume and control my life,
Bury all my feelings to unearth when I'm older.

But why do I care?
It literally makes zero impact
on my life unless I let it.
I'm annoyed at myself,
I can't believe it's taken me
this long to finally get it.

I need to let it all go.
People's opinion of me
is no longer my concern.
I don't need to defend myself to people,
Who are hateful
and will never learn.

I'm going to stop caring about your opinions,
And start living for me.
I feel like I've unlocked a super power.
I finally feel free.

balance

I knew I was struggling when
simply living was starting to feel like a challenge.
I was so mentally exhausted that I could
no longer keep up with this lifestyle,
And my mind was in desperate need of balance.

I'll be honest, there were times when
my mental health was hanging by a rope.
I was pushing my way through, ignoring the red flags.
Refusing to admit that I was struggling to cope.

But I made myself a promise.
This is going to be the year I put my own needs before others.
I want to learn who is the person inside,
sift through the dark and ugly,
Unravel all the covers.

So, for the first time in a long time
I gave myself permission to have a break.
Mainly, for my mental health's sake.
I needed to just shut off, go offline.
Seek comfort from within, get lost in my own mind.

And it honestly helped a lot.
I've been doing a lot of internal healing.
I've been working on myself,
going through the bad and ugly.
And discovering new feelings.

Be kind to yourself,
You're doing your best.
Be gentle and understanding,
Allow your mind to heal and rest.
If you fail or struggle in life,
I promise you, it's not the end.
Be there for yourself,
Because ultimately you're your own best friend.

confidence grows

Take the first step to working on yourself,
And watch as your confidence grows.
When a person focuses on themselves and their worth,
That's when their true strength shows.

humans make mistakes*

Society puts so much pressure on being perfect,
When humans are inherently flawed.
As humans we all make mistakes and do things we regret,
Yet somehow this is something we choose to ignore.
Ask yourself this, how many of you
have never made a mistake?
Never done anything you regret,
never had bad thoughts, negative judgements,
Or had something unkind to say?
Most of us can't relate, and that's okay.
Normalise being human.
And what I mean by this is normalising
making mistakes and learning from them
Because that's how us humans grow.
Making mistakes in itself doesn't make you a bad person,
it's how you behave after it,
that really shows
the kind of person you are.
Do you continue to make the same mistakes,
or change your behaviour to see how far
you have come.
Instead of hiding behind your mistakes,
it's healthier to acknowledge what you've done.
Because then you can fix it and
ultimately that's how you grow.

*Friendly reminder that you don't need to be perfect,
it's okay to be human,
Just something I thought you should know.

i'm pretty

I'm **pretty** confident there's many parts of me
    I've yet to explore,
And I'm **pretty** curious to see what they are
    and learn some more.
I'm **pretty** fascinated by the human mind,
    it's capable of so much,
I'm **pretty** excited to turn these thoughts into words
    and see how many people they touch.

I'd say I'm **pretty** strong, I've been hurt a lot but still wake up
    and choose love.
I'm **pretty** proud of myself for making it this far, I've managed
    to rise above.
Sometimes I'm **pretty** saddened by how society views me
    and my worth.
I find beauty and societal standards **pretty** strange,
    surely there's more to life on this earth?

I'm **pretty** headstrong and feel like I know
    who I am most of the time.
But sometimes I get **pretty** doubtful and question
    if I can make it in the big city?
I'm a **pretty** impulsive, inquisitive, confused human being,
But mostly I'm **pretty** certain that there's more to me
    than simply being **pretty**.

Strong ♥
♥ Independent
Caring ♥

chasing a feeling

My whole life I've been chasing a rare feeling,
A moment when I feel blissfully carefree.
When my happiness is so abundant and contagious
it just oozes from within me.
The smile on my face is so big it hurts.
I'm completely and utterly present.
In this moment nothing else matters.
And everything in life is pleasant.

chasing your dreams

Do you want to know the truth?
Chasing your dreams is hard.
It's full of sacrifices and heartbreak,
And feeling like you're not getting very far.
You spend a lot of nights
crying yourself to sleep,
Scared you made the wrong decision.
Surrounded by people waiting to see you fail.
And the life you dream of gets harder to envision.
Chasing your dreams isn't sunshine and rainbows,
It's tough and lonely.
It's not an overnight success.
The hard work pays off slowly.

When it gets tough I need to remind myself that
life's too short.
And I refuse to live an unfulfilled life.
I don't want to lie on my deathbed thinking about
the life I could've lived.
I refuse to give up this fight.

It's getter harder to believe in myself,
But I am all I have and I want to live a life I choose.
It's hard to see it now, but I know
one day all my dreams will come true,
I'll be the person I've always wanted to be
and everyone will see what I always knew.

I have to believe in myself,
I just have to make it through.

find myself again

There are days where you
find yourself completely lost and alone,
And the battle to keep moving forward
feels so incredibly long.
It feels like you've been here
so many times before.
But you no longer have the energy
to keep fighting and be strong.

Sometimes existing feels exhausting.
The world doesn't stop
just because you're in pain.
Life feels like an endless loop,
And no matter how hard you try,
things never seem to change.
When I'm in this mindset,
It's hard to think another way.
It's hard to be positive,
And hope that things will be okay.

But the truth is I am all I have.
And it's in these times that
I need to learn to be my own friend,
To hold my hand while I pick up the pieces,
Until I slowly find myself again.
It's going to be a painful and difficult process,
But I'll be stronger for it in the end.

perfection

I've hit rock bottom again,
Feels like all the work
I've put in has been lost.
I've suppressed my problems for so long,
But at what cost?

I'm realising that fighting
your inner demons,
A battle that at times
feels tiring and long,
Doesn't make you weak,
The same way being stoic
doesn't make you strong.

We're just human at the end of the day
Which means we're inherently flawed.
I thought striving for perfection
would make life easier.
But it just left me
feeling like a fraud.

Surprisingly, the thing that set me free
Was raw, unfiltered, brutal honesty.
Once I acknowledged my flaws,
it was like I could finally breathe.
I was no longer controlled by perfection,
I was just me.

manifesting me

I'm going to create this image of myself.
And she is going to be perfect,
she is going to be everything I want to be.

And I'm going to work hard and manifest,
Until one day that image
becomes me.

prove them wrong

People will underestimate you.
Try to convince you you're wrong.
And it will be frustrating
because you can't prove your potential yet,
But deep down you know where you belong.

Stay silent and stay focused,
Let the work and dedication be your distraction.
Because when results start coming in
it'll do all the talking for you,
And that will be the ultimate satisfaction.

moon

Even in my darkest moments, you helped me see the light.
You'd laugh with me through the pain,
Keep me company on my loneliest nights.
We were just two kids,
So scared and afraid of the future.
But you made the dark days easier,
Thank you, my friend, my sister,
partner in crime and former tutor.

Thank you for always saying yes
to my crazy ideas,
For accepting me as I am.
For listening and validating my feelings,
And even when I doubted myself,
always believing that I can.

I watch how far we've come and it fills me with pride.
It all seems surreal because we know
it hasn't always been an easy ride,
At times it's been painful and scary,
But it's also been an absolute joy thanks to having you by my side.

You're the moon to my sun,
Our friendship has shaped the person I've become.
Let's continue to keep learning and growing together,
And embrace whatever may come.

confidence

Once you realise confidence isn't a look:
It's a feeling.
You can start working on yourself
And begin the healing.

growth

Last year was the first time
I took on the world
completely by myself.

I was going through life alone,
no one to depend on,
only relying on myself for help.
And was it scary?
Yes.
But looking back on it
I think it's safe to say,
that it was all for the best.

I look at the past year
I look at the growth
I look at how much I've changed.
Every little step led me to the person I am now,
and honestly,
I wouldn't have it any other way.
Sure, there were times when
I struggled and life got really tough,
But I proved to myself that I can come out of it
and that I am more than enough.

I've always doubted my abilities,
was always the first to bring myself down,
But someway, somehow,
I managed to turn my life around.

I wish I could go back to my old self,
and talk to that 14-year-old kid.
Show her all the things she goes on to achieve.
You did it, you really did.

it's not your fault

After all these years you still
can't shake the unsettling feeling,
You carry the guilt with you
everywhere you go.
But I need you to understand
that none of it was your fault,
It's time to   let   the trauma   go.

see myself differently

I'm starting to see myself differently.
I can see how much I've grown.
I finally understand all the things
my past self did for me.
Which is why I now choose to
cherish this body I call home.

I'M FINE

(resolution / affirmations / intention)

i love myself

To love myself,
I have to be honest.
I need to accept myself

          as   I   am.

I need to make myself that promise.

I need to acknowledge every
broken,
      ugly,
           flawed
               part
               of
               me
and embrace them
with open arms.
Nurture them,
give them the care and attention
they deserve.
And protect them from any harm.

I need to look at myself in the mirror
in my most raw form.
And tell myself every single day,
        I choose you.

I choose to invest my
time, energy and love,
Because I think you're worthy of love, too.

Confidence isn't feeling great
when life's perfect.

Confidence is believing in myself
when I have nothing.

Confidence is knowing my worth
isn't determined by external factors,

And that I matter
and am worth something.

Confidence, like any thing in life, is a skill.
I didn't learn how to read and write in a day.
So, how can I expect confidence to be that way?

It's
something I have to practise,
something I have to invest in,
something I have to believe
with every part of my being
and put to the ultimate test.

So, I'll keep practising, until one day,
just like speaking,
it'll become second nature.

To be confident I need to get to know myself,
learn and discover every aspect of what makes me, me.
Explore, experiment, ask myself questions.
Keep growing until I fall in love with the person I see.

The biggest mistake I made was running from myself,
I'd mask, distract and wonder why my efforts in
finding confidence felt so empty.
Truth is, I can't find the love inside by looking elsewhere.
It's exhausting and unhealthy.

The more I learn about myself,
the more self-assured I feel.
My thoughts, experiences, humour, interests
All say something unique about me.

I have a whole lifetime to discover myself.
I have the power to be whoever I want to be.

I'm rooting for myself every single day
because I am my own best friend.

I'm manifesting the best things in life
because I deserve it.

I'm feeding myself nutritious food
to become healthy and strong.

I'm educating myself so that
I can best understand who I am.

I'm challenging myself beyond my comfort zone
to see my potential.

I think highly of myself

to show myself I deserve respect.

I allow myself to be emotional

because I understand I'm human.

I love myself

because I care about myself.

I embrace every part of myself
because they tell stories,
and all those stories
add up to me.

I'm proud of who I am
because I've worked hard
to feel this free.

A complex, curious, spontaneous, educated,
passionate, caring human being.

And against all the odds,
I have well and truly
fallen in love with myself.

purpose

We're taught that we need to have purpose in life.
That we must provide something of value to have worth.
So we beat ourselves up trying to find meaning,
And spend our whole life questioning our existence on earth.

But there's no truth to any of this,
It's just expectations demanded from society.
We feel like we need to be something to prove ourselves,
And this pressure riddles our life with anxiety.

But you need to know that none of it matters,
The conditioning will try to control you
but you have to resist.
Understand that your value comes from
                              being, living and loving,
You don't need to earn
your right to exist.

one shot at life

You only get one shot at life.
Yet we spend so much of it
picking ourselves apart,
focusing all our energy onto our flaws,
that we give up before we even start.

I've heard the excuse 'well it'll never happen'
or 'I wasn't destined for that life.'
But how can you be so sure
when you've never even tried?
We live in an age where
there's so much opportunity
yet few take advantage of it.
Give it a shot – go out of your comfort zone –
you might be surprised.

I spent so much of my life doubting myself,
telling myself that I wasn't good or talented enough,
People would tell me to *just go for it*
yet I'd still come up with every excuse under the sun.
Why do we do that?
Why do we put ourselves down so much?

So, this year I made it my mission to end that,
put aside all my fears and just go for it.
I was done with restricting myself.
I'm not going to settle with being comfortable anymore.
And honestly, it was the best thing I ever did.

It's only when I stopped
and asked myself *what* is it that I want?
that I started to actually live my life.
You spend so much of your life
living up to these expectations
that you forget what you want,
you become numb inside.
This past year I've laughed, danced, smiled, cried,
I no longer feel the need to hide.

From experiencing heartbreak,
failure, painful late nights,
to running around a field in the middle of July.
I took a risk, went with my gut instinct
and things turned out fine,
and I know that deep, deep down,
things are going to be alright.
It's just a matter of time.

You shouldn't stop living in the face of fear,
You shouldn't stop chasing the dream
just because the roads aren't clear.
You work hard and you push through it,
What's important is that you're here.
So make the most of that –
go out there and do what it is that you love,
stop coming up with a million excuses
and telling yourself you're not good enough.
Things aren't handed to you,
you work hard and you go get it.
Embrace it with both arms and go chase it.

Yes, you're going to make mistakes,
and yes, there will be times
when you doubt yourself, second guess your choices,
make yourself small with self-hate.
But ask yourself this?
Wouldn't you rather try and know what happens –
than live your whole life knowing you left it too late?
For one moment just learn to let go,
and put your happiness in the hands of fate.
The chance is now, it's always now.
If you're not happy and feel trapped,
stop and start afresh somehow.

Go on road trips, talk to people, dance at festivals,
Learn about people's stories, ask questions, feed your soul.

There's so much happiness out there –
you just need to be brave enough to see it.
Work hard and the results will follow.
But you need to start in order to believe it.
Wake up every morning feeling passionate and carefree,
knowing nine to five routine isn't the only way to be.
There's so much out there,
an abundance of opportunity,
don't let it go to waste
because you were too scared to dream.

This year I got to feel, like *really* feel,
understand who I am as a person and connect with people.
I feel like I actually have a voice now
and I use it to talk about things that matter.
I'm finally doing something I love,
Here's to the next chapter!

three little words

We wait a lifetime to hear those
three words that never come.
Those three words are so simple
yet hold so much weight.
They have the power
to wash away all our pain,
Make us go from feeling worthless
to something great.

We work our whole lives,
In the hope that someday
someone will see our worth.
We forget who we need to hear it from most,
The one person on this earth,

It's you.

I hope you're
proud of yourself.

your own best friend

We spend too much time wanting to be someone else,
We should focus that energy on being our own friend.
Once we learn to appreciate ourselves and see our worth,
We'll realise we're all we needed in the end.

change

I used to be scared of change,
I would cling onto everything I knew
even if it wasn't always the best for me.
I would clutch onto familiarity
because I was scared of the   unknown,
But with time I learned to let go
and left the rest to destiny.

By learning to let go I got to see a whole new world,
Full of possibilities, new doors leading to new   lanes.
It opened my eyes to the point where I'm no longer scared –
But actually, embrace change.

Change has challenged and shaped
The person I am today,
It has taught me so many lessons.
Yes, things can go wrong but they can also go really great!
Instead of worrying about the future
I need to learn to focus on the present.

Change leads to growth,
And I can't wait to see the person I turn out to   be.
So, I'm going to trust the unknown, however scary,
And embrace all of life's possibilities.

so many possibilities

When I was younger I always thought
you had to be one kind of person.
That you grow up and find your thing
and that's who you will be for the rest of your life.
But this notion never really sat well with me.
And honestly, caused me a great deal of mental strife.

'Cause you see the more
I challenged the idea of who I am,
the more I discovered parts of me
I never knew existed.
I've always wanted to be so many different things,
but for some reason I've always resisted.

Maybe it was my lack of confidence.
I didn't even want to try 'cause,
what if people laugh at me?
I would deny myself
the different lives I could live.
Because I was too afraid people would see

> me fail,
> be awkward,
> or look like
> I'm trying too hard.

But if I keep stifling my growth,
I'm not gonna exactly get very far.

I remember hearing someone say
that you can wake up one day and
decide to be a completely different person.

Like literally, there's nothing stopping you.

And it was like a light switch went on,
'Cause now the possibilities for me were endless,
I no longer had to choose
Between one thing that would define me.
I am a multitude of choices
and none of them confine me.

I have unleashed
all the beautiful possibilities,
And finally I see.

Oh how wonderful
it feels to just live,
and be this carefree.

live life to the fullest

If you're not going to live your life to the fullest
then what's the point?
And by that, I don't mean making
some crazy life-changing decision on the spot.
I mean making the most of every moment you've got.
You existing and being alive is such a rare thing
and it's crazy to live life as if it's not.

Tell the people that mean the most to you
that you love them,
Show the people in your life
how much you care.
Be bold about your passions
and the things that make you happy,
Express your personality
through the clothes you wear.

Romanticise and appreciate the little things in life.
For those moments create the big picture.
Allow yourself to be honest with your feelings
and be brave enough to reveal them.
Life doesn't have to be one linear path, it can be a mixture.

Life is too short to hide who you are.
You owe it to yourself to live a full life.
Empower yourself to make your own choices.
That's when you'll finally start feeling alive.

mind

I've never understood why people are so
obsessed with how they look on the outside,
When the most beautiful part about being human
is our incredible mind.

It tells an infinite number of stories,
Turns ideas into reality.
Absorbs complex information,
helps us better understand society,
learn concepts and pick up skills.
It has the power to turn every
'no, you can't' to 'yes, I will!'

It strings words into sentences
that make people feel understood and alive.
It's a place where we can keep our deepest secrets,
A safe space for us to hide.

It lets our imagination run wild,
And creates worlds with no boundaries or limits,
It's the place where we can truly be ourselves,
A place that embraces our soul and spirit.

It can turn negative thoughts into positive ones.
It has the power to mend and heal.
It can transform our everyday into something spectacular.
When we discover all the things we can feel.

So, I never understood why we're so fixated on the outer shell.
Why do we care so much for the skin and bones?
It all feels so surface level and empty,
When you realise that inside you lives your true home.

daily reminder

You're not difficult.   You have trauma.

You're not angry.   You're in pain.

You're not a bad person.   You're human.

You will no longer be controlled by guilt or shame.

You're not emotional.   You have emotions.

You are not defined by anyone.   Other than yourself.

You're not boring.   You have boundaries.

It's not selfish to do what's best for your mental health.

You're not a burden.   You just haven't found people
who understand you.

Instead of worrying about
whether they like you,   ask yourself if you even like
them?

Whenever you find yourself questioning or doubting yourself,

Take a step back and repeat these words again.

i got help

I've been taking some time out to work on myself.
I talk about how we should strive to be the
best version of ourselves we can possibly be.

I'm afraid I failed to take my own advice.

For years I was consumed by creating
this perfect, happy image of myself,
So, I often failed to recognise
How I really felt inside.
In every picture I'd have the biggest smile –
you'd never even question it.

You'd never see when I was alone
All by myself, I'd just cry.
I cried all the time.

For years I denied
        how I felt,
Didn't want to be defined
        by this feeling.
I refused to be caged
        by my own thoughts
Always pushing myself
        to get through it.

Distracting myself with work, friends, uni,
Never really acknowledging
that when it came down to it,
I was never truly happy.

This feeling would cling to me,
And slowly pull me down.
I became unmotivated, lifeless,
my mind would no longer want to create.
I would spend months isolating myself,
filling myself with angst, frustration,
debilitated by my own self-hate.

And it slowly drove me insane.

The truth is, I'm just someone who's having
A really tough time loving herself,
    and a little over a month ago
    I was starting to get really bad again.
I was truly at a low point,
all passion, all motivation had gone,
I didn't know what to do, so I confided in a friend.

After a long chat I took a moment to think.
Things slowly started to make sense.
The truth was that I had to accept ...

                                    That I had a problem,
And only then would all this sadness end.

If I want to get better
I need to start with myself.
So that's what I did,
I took the first step,
admitted I had a problem
and I finally sought help.

Honestly, I don't know what
I'm going to do next,
but I do know that the right path
doesn't always come easily.
Here's to giving myself the best chance,
here's to working on being the best version of myself
I can possibly be.

power

I realised it's all in my mindset,
That's what will determine the life I will lead.
I thought I needed to succumb
to their demands or I'll be alone,
But the truth is
I am all I need.

The power has always been in my hands,
But people have convinced me to give it away.
They beat me down till I had no self-esteem left,
And brainwashed me into
thinking things won't change ...
But that ends today.

I will be the hero in my own story,
I will fight for my power till the end of time.
I will be strong and stand up for myself,
And own what was rightfully mine.

note to self

Work so hard pursuing your dreams,
You have no time to be jealous or compare.

Surround yourself with genuine, good people,
Who support you, love you and care.

Remember to always take care of yourself,
But have enough love to spare.

You're as good as the energy you put out in the world,
Be kind, be present, be fair.

the answer is you

You're putting too much pressure on yourself
to find the perfect job, relationship, body.
And in the fear of sounding really sappy,
I'm just gonna be real with you here,
None of that stuff is going to make you happy.

You know what will?

You.

If you allow yourself to.

whole on my own

It's funny.
When I started doing things alone
and spent more time with myself,
I started to realise how great I am,
and it improved my mental health.

It made me realise that all the self-hate was taught.
I was made to feel that way by others.
I want to apologise to my younger self for giving in to it all.
I will never allow my judgement to be influenced by another.
I now realise that I'm whole on my own,
I have value and worth and I'm protecting my energy.
I decide the terms on how I live my life.
And the self-loathing is a distant memory.

i'm fine

I walk down the streets aimlessly, free,
I walk knowing there's no place I need to be.
I'm a tiny dot in the great big city
and for some reason
that makes me feel safe.
Like all my problems are small
and things are going to be okay.

I do things only for me now.
And life just feels a lot easier somehow.

I rest my head in my own home
and go to sleep in peace.
Staring at the fairy lights
and scented candles that smell
so sweet.
I find myself enjoying
all of life's little delicacies.

Things really did get better with time.
I can honestly, wholeheartedly say,
I'm fine.

WHERE TO START IF YOU'RE LOOKING FOR FURTHER HELP

As much as I am a big believer in the healing power of self-expression and reflection, and encourage you to write your own poetry, produce your own creative work and talk with trusted friends – sometimes, it isn't quite enough.

If you've been struggling with your mental health or have been affected by any of the topics covered in this book, like depression, anxiety, self-image and gaslighting, there are resources you can go to for help. No one should have to suffer silently and it's time for the stigma and shame around our mental health and emotional wellbeing to end.

Below are a few places you can find help and resources to support your mental health and wellbeing. It is not an exhaustive list, but it could be a great starting point to gather some useful information that can help you on your journey.

Ditch the Label

forums.ditchthelabel.org
A global youth charity who can help with bullying, mental health, relationships, identity and the tough stuff in-between.

They can provide free toolkits and self-help, plus access to confidential advice from trained mentors who have or are going through similar issues.

Headspace

headspace.org.au

Mental health support, resources and advice for young Australians aged 12-25.

Kids Help Phone

kidshelpphone.ca

Call 1 800 668 6868 or text CONNECT to 686868.

Available 24 hours a day to Canadians aged 5-29 who want confidential and anonymous care from professional counsellors.

Mind

mind.org.uk

0300 123 3393 (Monday to Friday, 9 a.m.–6 p.m.)

If you're living with a mental health problem, need support or advice on treatment, or want to support someone who does, Mind is an organisation that can help those based in England and Wales.

MindLine Trans +

mindlinetrans.org.uk

0300 330 5468 (Mondays and Fridays, 8 p.m.–midnight)

A confidential, emotional mental health support helpline for people who identify as transgender, agender, gender fluid and non-binary in the UK.

National Suicide Prevention Lifeline

800 273 8255

A 24/7 helpline for confidential emotional support to those in crisis who are based in the US.

Nightline

nightline.ac.uk/want-to-talk/

Any university student in the UK can contact Nightline at their institution, every night of term, via their website. Nothing is too big or small to contact Nightline about – whatever's troubling a caller, Nightline is there to listen.

Samaritans

samaritans.org

116 123 (24 hours, 365 days)

A 24-hour helpline offering emotional support for anyone feeling distressed or struggling to cope. Texting for deaf callers: 0330 094 5717.

UNICEF

voicesofyouth.org/mental_health_communicating_what_you_need

Connect with a worldwide community about mental health, what matters to you and how you really feel. UNICEF works in over 190 countries to protect the rights and wellbeing of every child. Voices of Youth is their online media platform for youth, by youth, and features free mental health resources.

ACKNOWLEDGEMENTS

Thank you to my supportive friends and family for always being there for me and helping me navigate life.

Thank you to my agent, Zach Brown, and the team at Independent Talent for believing in me and being a constant source of support and encouragement.

Thank you to my editor, Amandeep, for always being so passionate about my poetry and working tirelessly to make this book happen.

Thank you to the incredibly talented Shamima for bringing the poetry to life with your impactful illustrations.

Finally, and most importantly, thank you to my readers, fans and supporters for changing my life and making me believe things get better. This book exists thanks to you. I hope it can give you the love, understanding and support you have always shown me.

ABOUT THE AUTHOR

Taz Alam (AKA ClickForTaz) is a British content creator best known for her hugely popular YouTube channel. Growing up in Cardiff and graduating with a degree in Law, Taz quickly found a platform on YouTube to share her spoken-word poetry, which to her surprise rapidly gained in popularity. Encouraged by her dedicated audience, Taz now posts a mix of wholesome lifestyle and travel vlogs, comedy and challenges. Taz has amassed tens of millions of views since starting her channel in 2015 and has quickly become one of the most prominent YouTubers in the UK.

 YouTube

@ClickForTaz